Furniture Making
A FOUNDATION COURSE

Furniture Making

A FOUNDATION COURSE

John Bullar

Fox
Chapel Publishing

1970 Broad Street • East Petersburg, PA 17520
www.FoxChapelPublishing.com

Furniture Making: A Foundation Course is an original work, first published in 2008 by The Guild of Master Craftsmen Publications Ltd. The patterns contained herein are copyrighted by the author. Readers may make three copies of these patterns for personal use. The patterns themselves, however, are not to be duplicated for resale or distribution under any circumstances. Any such copying is a violation of copyright law.

All illustrations by the author except those on the following pages:
Simon Rodway: 118, 123, 131, 139, 144, 151, 169 (bottom), 177 (bottom)
Ian Hall: 169 (top), 177 (top)

ISBN 978-1-56523-380-5

Bullar, John, 1954-

Furniture making : a foundation course / John Bullar. -- Lewes, East
Sussex : Guild of Master Craftsman Publications ; East Petersburg,
PA : dist. in the U.S. by Fox Chapel Publishing, c2008.

 p. ; cm.
 ISBN: 978-1-56523-380-5
 Issued in England as "Cabinetmaking: a foundation course".
 Includes index.

 1. Furniture making--Patterns. 2. Furniture making--Technique.
 I. Guild of Master Craftsmen. II. Title. III. Cabinetmaking: a
foundation course.

TT195 .B85 2008
684.1/04--dc22   0801

To learn more about the other great books from Fox Chapel Publishing, or to find a retailer near you, call toll-free 1-800-457-9112 or visit us at **www.FoxChapelPublishing.com**.

Note to Authors: We are always looking for talented authors to write new books in our area of woodworking, design, and related crafts. Please send a brief letter describing your idea to Peg Couch, Acquisition Editor, 1970 Broad Street, East Petersburg, PA 17520.

Printed in China
10 9 8 7 6 5 4 3 2 1

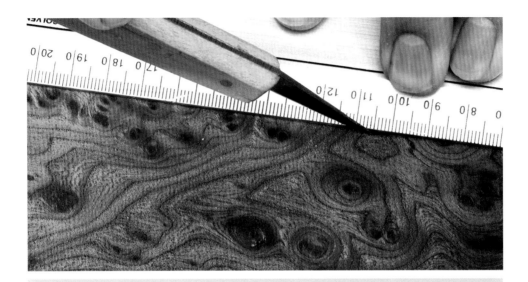

Although care has been taken to ensure that the imperial measurements are true and accurate, they are only conversions from metric; they have been rounded up or down to the nearest $\frac{1}{16}$in, or to the nearest convenient equivalent in cases where the metric measurements themselves are only approximate. When following the projects, use either the metric or the imperial measurements; do not mix units.

SYMBOLS USED IN THE PROJECTS

The following symbols are used in the projects section to indicate levels of skill required and proficiency with which tools is needed.

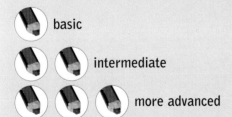 basic

intermediate

more advanced

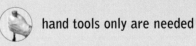 hand tools only are needed

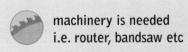 machinery is needed
i.e. router, bandsaw etc

CUTTING LISTS

The first six projects include a cutting list to help beginners get started. Buy all wood over size then cut and plane to an accurate fit by directly marking one piece against another. Later projects (7–10) omit a cutting list as the maker will have gained enough practice to adapt the dimensions as required.

Contents

PART TWO PROJECTS

Foreword

Working with wood runs through John Bullar's blood – his grandfather was a cabinetmaker and his father a keen amateur. Since he was eleven he has been making things from wood and reading about furniture-making. Some of the many books he devoured as he grew up were, of course, 'the Bible' for all furniture-makers Joyce's *The Technique of Furniture Making* and others by Krenov. So, to be writing his own articles, and this book, was a natural progression.

John has been writing for *Furniture & Cabinetmaking* magazine for well over five years and I know many readers have completed their own 'apprenticeship' through John's clear, succinct writing and photography which conveys a very evident passion for his subject. I am sure that many more will find this book a real asset in the workshop as a reference and indeed as another tool in their armoury. There is plenty of variety in the projects, something to suit everyone's ability and to stretch your making skills a little further, finding something new along the way. So get out your plane and set out on a new voyage of discovery.

Colin Eden-Eadon
Editor, *Furniture & Cabinetmaking*

Introduction

Wounded in the Great War, my grandfather Ajax Bullar was sent home from the trenches to train as a cabinetmaker. Nearly a century later, some of the furniture he made as a disabled apprentice is still used and valued by members of my family. Nowadays, it makes sound environmental sense to turn good wood into fine furniture that will last long and be appreciated for generations, whether by your own family or your customer's.

This book starts by helping you select hardwood that will look beautiful and behave well, then choosing the right tools to work it into furniture projects. It is best to start with a few simple tools of high quality rather than complex apparatus that promises miracles. As well as helping to budget, buying equipment in stages means you get to know each tool before acquiring another. If you start with good hand tools, you can experience every process in close-up, feeling the nature of the wood and the response of a cutting edge. Different makers have different views of when to use hand tools instead of machines, although most agree it is better to learn a technique with hand tools first; that way you will understand the job more deeply if you later use a machine. Hand tools are also more versatile, so if you come to a task the machine cannot do, your hand-tool skills can solve the problem.

As well as their methods of work, makers depend on their eyes to avoid flaws in construction. What is visible to you depends on your eyesight and the lighting. If like me you need glasses, they must have safety lenses that focus sharply at working distance. Establish a good lighting set up on the workplace by positioning the bench under a window or angling a desk lamp to highlight details.

The right approach to accuracy means parts will fit together neatly and firmly. I prefer to measure in millimetres because it helps me think small, but most critical dimensions are marked directly from wood to wood without using measurements. Accurate work takes time and this is time well spent rather than time that might be wasted later, trying to fix errors made in haste. Speed improves with practice while quality is a priority for makers at every level, so give yourself time to learn cabinetmaking.

John Bullar, 2007

Part One Tools and techniques

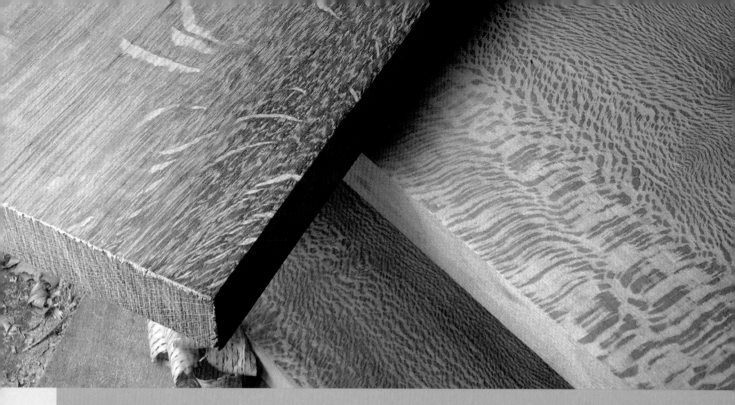

Choosing and storing timber

Decent wood is essential for furniture-making, so learning the basics of choosing and storing timber is vital. By choosing wood carefully, you are more likely to be satisfied with the process and the end results.

FINDING WOOD

There is a whole spectrum of wood suppliers out there – ranging between the big DIY supermarket chains, the specialist timber merchants and the local tree surgeon who occasionally hires a bandsaw mill. The DIY market mostly sells softwoods, often damp and not of the quality that you will require. Small dealers may sell some interesting hardwoods, often complete with waney edges and bark. Highly figured and rippled woods can look spectacular but take more care to work successfully. Adverts in magazines or a search on the internet will lead you to hardwood specialists, while small local suppliers are more likely to be found listed in directories such as the *Yellow Pages*.

ABOVE Medullary ray figuring on the face of quarter-sawn oak (left) and London plane (right).

WHICH WOODS?

Hardwoods are mostly, but not always, harder than softwoods. The actual distinction is that hardwoods come from broad-leaf trees like oak or beech, while softwoods are from needled trees like pine or larch. The important difference to furniture-makers is that hardwoods cut cleanly and accurately and provide a better finish than softwoods.

Oak is a traditional favourite – it is coarse-grained like ash and elm. While strong, it splits relatively easily along the grain. Hardwoods cropped on a large scale, like American oak, grow in forests where they shoot up tall and straight competing for daylight. British oaks felled for road-widening schemes are likely to be lone trees with short trunks and many low branches. The resulting timber can be interesting but is wasteful, so hard to find commercially.

Sycamore, maple or beech can be used in contact with food. Fine hardwoods like walnut are several times more expensive but for a small project, the cost is less significant compared to the investment of time. One highly prized 'softwood' is yew, that is harder than most hardwoods, but it is poisonous. Another is cedar because of its lasting qualities and fresh scent.

JARGON BUSTING

timber (or lumber) – wood as a raw material

1 A forest oak grows a tall, straight trunk, competing to get its foliage in the daylight.

2 This roadside oak has a short trunk and tried to grow lower limbs where the daylight is plentiful.

TIMBER CONDITION

Wood is normally sold as flat boards. These have been sliced from tree trunks, then either kilned or air-dried. The whole process is known as 'timber conversion'. Think of the fibres in a tree trunk as a bundle of fine tubes carrying water as sap from the roots up to the leaves. The tree's growth is seasonal, so each year a new ring of fibres forms just beneath the bark producing more sapwood. After several years being covered by successive outer rings, each ring of fibres stops carrying sap and converts to heartwood. This hardens with natural preservatives and provides the tree with strength.

When the tree is felled, there is much water stored in the fibres. As the wood dries and the moisture content falls below 30% – i.e. the weight of water is 30% of the weight of dry wood – it starts to change in shape. The cut ends of the fibres are like open tubes, so these dry quickest. As water is lost, each fibre shrinks in thickness and slightly in length. The wood at the ends tries to make itself narrower than the rest – so something has to give. The result is splits, or checks in the surface. You can see the effect as radial cracks across the ends of logs that are left to dry out.

To avoid cracks propagating along the timber, the converter's first task is to slice the trunk into boards before it shrinks. A common system is to use a large bandsaw mill that moves on rails, while the trunk lies between them in a fixed position, being sliced up like bacon. Boards cut this way are referred to as 'through and through' or 'flat' sawn. The face grain shows elliptical and U-shaped patterns. You can see this easily by looking at the sawn ends, where you will see arcs that were part of the rings in the trunk. Wide boards from near the middle of the trunk have short arcs, while narrower boards from the outside have long arcs stretched across the board width and are more liable to cupping. Sometimes the converter will manoeuvre timber to saw as many wide boards as possible close to a line

3

4

through the centre of the trunk. This is known as quarter-sawing. The face pattern is straight-grained while the ends show short sections of growth rings at right angles to face. There is more wastage and more work producing quarter-sawn timber, so it is more expensive to buy. However, the wood is particularly stable and the medullary rays give quarter-sawn hardwoods, such as oak and plane, very distinctive appearances.

The narrow strip at the centre of the tree where the pith lies is normally wasted. Dark-coloured hardwoods have pale sapwood that is softer. This may also need to be discarded for fine furniture, but some makers use the variations creatively. For special small pieces of furniture, it is possible to quarter-saw wood from logs on a small scale using a workshop bandsaw, but this is impractical for any quantity.

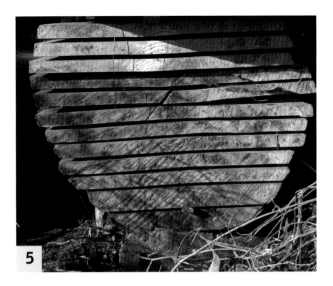

5

6

7

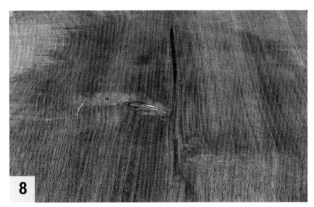

8

9

3 Oak trees felled in a plantation to make room for new growth.

4 A bandsaw mill slices an oak trunk into boards.

5 After sawing into boards, the timber converter stacks them for drying with spaces, supported by 'stickers'.

6 Quarter-sawn timber has short rings visible on the end grain, perpendicular to the face. The fine horizontal lines in the end grain are medullary rays.

7 Quarter-sawing on a small scale in the workshop.

8 The pith line along the centre of a walnut board.

9 A waney-edged board from a tall, straight oak, the brown heartwood surrounded by pale sapwood and bark.

JARGON BUSTING

stickers – strips of wood used to separate boards when drying.
moisture content – water content as a percentage by weight of the dry wood.

KILNED OR AIR-DRIED?

A drying method often used by traditional timber converters is to stack the boards in an outdoor pile, with thin softwood stickers separating them. This allows breezes to waft through, removing moisture from all the surfaces. The resulting timber, known as 'air-dried', is still preferred by many makers who appreciate its working qualities.

Air-drying in quantity uses up a lot of space because it is a slow process that requires a year's drying time for each inch thickness. The final moisture content is typically 15–18%. Some further slow drying indoors is usually required to take the moisture content below 12%, suitable for use in a warm house. A dehumidifier in the workshop can accelerate the process.

Commercial timber converters more commonly stack the timber in large insulated containers, with warm air circulated by fans. The process, known as kiln-drying, accelerates the time from years to weeks, producing a typical level around 10%, suitable for use in a centrally heated house. Sometimes kiln-drying is not correctly controlled and the board develops long end splits. If these are of a finger-length, they are accepted as normal but much longer and you would expect the price to be reduced for waste. Surface cracks or checks partway along the board suggest case hardening – a serious kilning fault that also creates honeycomb fissures inside the wood.

Once wood has dried, it readily soaks up moisture again by extracting water vapour from the air, until it reaches equilibrium. When air is humid, the fibres in a dry board swell up, increasing its width, while in dry weather the board contracts in width. Making furniture that survives 'wood movement' like this is an essential skill for the maker.

10

ROUGH-SAWN OR PLANED?

After timber conversion, the rough-sawn surfaces may not be flat, due to different rates of drying, but they must be planed flat before use. While choosing boards, a maker needs to judge how thick they will be once one face is flattened and the other planed parallel to a uniform thickness. If the board is cut into small pieces before planing, most of the thickness can be conserved. However, if large boards are needed this may be a limitation.

Rough-sawn timber looks considerably different from planed. It has less figuring and is blander in colour. The dealer may allow you to hand-plane a patch near the end to obtain a better view. Or, you could buy ready-planed timber. This enables you to see the wood's colour and its figuring.

The disadvantage of buying planed timber is that it is often stored outside after kilning, therefore it re-absorbs moisture. If planed when damp, then allowed to dry a board may cup across its width or bow along its length after planing. Also the planer blades in sawmills see a lot of challenging work and may be blunt, resulting in pitted surfaces. You should be prepared to re-plane any boards you may buy after a few weeks in your dry workshop and allow for further loss of thickness accordingly.

TECHNICAL TIP

Wastage is an inevitable part of furniture-making and, typically, you need to allow for 30% loss when estimating a project – more if it is complex or the timber is highly figured. Boards cut from the same tree will match better so try to select from one batch. Buying wood is one of those times when you need to think on your feet and make a commitment. You need to put your hand in your pocket and buy really nice wood where and when you see it. I keep finding this out the hard way!

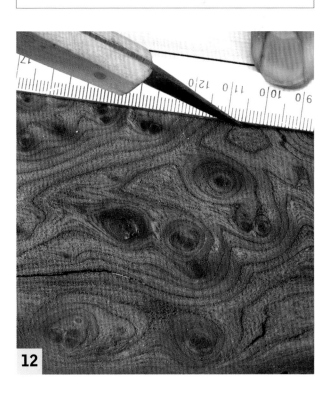

10 Rough-sawn boards stored under cover show undulations from uneven drying or stacking.

11 This kiln-dried oak was sealed at the end to minimize end-split wastage.

12 Burrs produce spectacular figuring which is mostly converted to veneers.

Planes

Planes are essential tools for the furniture-maker. In the past, makers used to plane large amounts of material by hand, but now they tend to have their timber machined first, reserving the hand plane for finer work.

Planes have ancient origins; even metal-framed models date back to the Roman Empire. In more recent history, the late Victorians made some excellent planes and this capability continued through the first half of the 20th century. Despite this, a few years ago it was difficult to obtain a good plane. Over the past decade plane-makers have dramatically improved the furniture-maker's choice. Now they produce extensive ranges of well-designed, high-quality bench planes, as well as more specialized shaping planes. The cost may be higher, but most furniture-makers agree it is worthwhile. With careful selection, buying used planes and restoring them is quite feasible.

ABOVE Planing with the grain, fibres are sheared at the cutting edge.

PLANE SIZES

Occasional users of planes tend to prefer the feel of small bench planes, typically a size 4. Larger models, particularly the well-made modern versions, contain a lot of metal and are heavy. However, the way a plane feels in the air is not relevant to how it is used. As long as you can lift it onto the wood at the beginning of a stroke and off again at the end, the extra weight will be borne by the timber. If you already have a small plane that you are comfortable with, but are considering upgrading to a superior model, it is well worth buying a larger plane so you will have a choice of sizes to use. The No. $5\frac{1}{2}$ is an excellent all-round tool.

The components of a bench plane

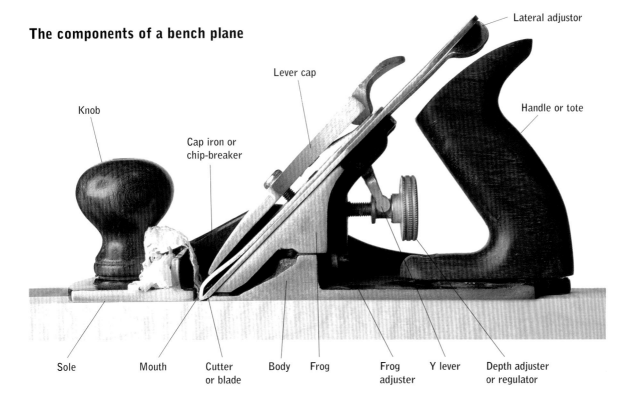

Lateral adjustor

Lever cap

Knob

Handle or tote

Cap iron or
chip-breaker

Sole Mouth Cutter
or blade Body Frog Frog
adjuster Y lever Depth adjuster
or regulator

1 A range of bench planes.

Typical Plane Sizes

Size No	Name	Plane Length	Blade Width
3	Small smoother	8in (200mm)	$1\frac{3}{4}$in (45mm)
4	Smoothing plane	$9\frac{1}{2}$in (240mm)	2in (50mm)
$4\frac{1}{2}$	Large smoother	$10\frac{3}{8}$in (264mm)	$2\frac{3}{8}$in (60mm)
5	Jack plane	14in (355mm)	2in (50mm)
$5\frac{1}{4}$	Junior jack	$11\frac{5}{8}$in (295mm)	$1\frac{3}{4}$in (45mm)
$5\frac{1}{2}$	Bench plane	$14\frac{3}{4}$in (375mm)	$2\frac{3}{8}$in (60mm)
6	Fore plane	18in (457mm)	$2\frac{3}{8}$in (60mm)
7	Jointer plane	22in (560mm)	$2\frac{3}{8}$in (60mm)

TECHNICAL TIP

The benefits of a longer sole are that it creates
straighter edges and flatter faces, while the weight
helps prevent it juddering. Some established makers do
most of their planing with a size 7, even on fine edges.

SHARPNESS

There is a subtle difference between sharpness and grinding angle. The front edge of the cutter forms a line where the wood that will become the shaving parts company from the wood that will stay behind on the surface. The thinner this line is, the sharper the edge and the easier the plane will glide along and the smoother the surface will be. The upper side of the cutter and the sole actually do all the work, making contact with the wood as the cutter pares away the shaving. The lower surface of the cutter – ground at an angle – just acts as a support to the cutting edge.

Consider how a knife or a chisel cuts. Both sides of the blade form a wedge between the job and the waste, forcing them apart, while the cutting edge severs through the fibres. If the blade is ground at a narrower angle, the wedge is more acute so it takes less force to drive the knife or chisel into the wood. However, in the case of a conventional plane, the upper side of the blade and the underside of sole form the wedge, and the angle between them is normally fixed at 45°. The underside of the blade does not touch the wood and, so long as it clears the surface, has no influence on the cut.

GRINDING ANGLES

A new plane cutter will usually come ready-ground with a bevel at 25–30°. Fitted on a plane frog at 45°, this leaves a quite useless air gap between the bevel and the wood, while the thinness of the steel will make the cutter's edge much more fragile than it needs to be.

Furniture-makers will often grind a secondary 'micro-bevel' on the cutter's edge, at a wider angle. The advantages are that you do not need to grind much metal away to sharpen the edge – and the edge will be much stronger – lasting longer before it needs re-sharpening. So long as the bevel is less than 45°, a wider grinding angle does not reduce the cutting action.

In the past, some makers took great pride in their skill of grinding bevel edges freehand. However, as this is essentially an engineering process, it makes more sense to use a honing guide – a cheap and simple wheel that clamps on the underside of a blade to control the angle. The upper side of a bench plane cutter must be flat and smooth so there is always contact with the underside of the chip-breaker. The edge of the chip-breaker itself must also be straight, but angled so it only makes contact at the front to prevent fibres becoming trapped and jamming the mouth. Once flattened and straightened, these surfaces rarely need attention.

STEEL CUTTERS

Modern cutter manufacturers use steels, hardened to around Rockwell 60–62 by the addition of high carbon content or by alloying with chromium, such as in A2 steel. Depending on the make of cutter, various methods of hammer forging and heat treatments are applied, including a super-cooled 'cryogenic' process. These aim to achieve the right degree of hardness without the brittleness that usually accompanies it. There are pros and cons to the various steels and processes used for cutters. Makers do not always agree which ones are best, although all good blades take a lot of work to make, so they are never cheap.

WHETSTONES

All blades wear down with use and eventually need sharpening. Rubbing the bevel edge of the cutter back and forth against a coarse stone – less than 1000 gauge – removes steel quickly, then using a fine stone – 4000 gauge or more – polishes the flat surface. The angle should exactly correspond with the bevel or the wider microbevel so the minimum amount of steel needs to be removed.

What modern cutter steels have in common is that they are all hard and grind slowly. It is very important to avoid heating the edge while you grind it and water is commonly used as a coolant and lubricant. Japanese waterstones consist of hard particles trapped in a soft base material or substrate. They are very effective on hard steels.

The disadvantage of Japanese waterstones is that they wear quickly to a hollow surface so the stones themselves need regular flattening if they are to produce straight-edged tools.

Diamond stones may sound exotic, but the price range is similar to waterstones. They consist of diamond grit trapped in a nickel coating on a steel base and are lubricated with water or cutting fluid. They grind quickly, staying flat and, with careful use, the diamonds stay attached for a long useful life. Diamond stones are dependable for someone starting out seriously in furniture-making.

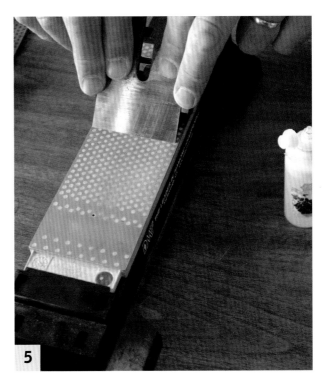

2 A honing guide controls the grinding angle for sharpening.

3 A poorly seated chip-breaker chokes up the mouth and prevents the plane cutting.

4 The chip-breaker needs a polished front and flat underside to seat on the cutter.

5 Water lubricates the diamond whetstone and flushes away steel particles.

6 The curved edge is just visible through the plane mouth.

7

AGAINST THE GRAIN

When planing a piece of wood, we want to shear through its fibres rather than lifting and tearing them from the surface. Sometimes it is clear this can be achieved by planing in one direction – namely 'with the grain'. In many cases, however, this is not possible or it is not obvious which direction is 'with the grain'. Examples can be found in rippled woods where the grain direction changes continuously and at joints where the maker brings together woods with different directions. In these cases, fibres might easily be prized out of the wood and peeled up ahead of the cutting edge resulting in a torn surface, especially if the edge is not sharp enough to shear them first.

PLANE MOUTH WIDTH

To reduce the tearing effect and make the plane more forgiving of fibre direction, a fine-mouth setting is used. As the cutter moves forwards, it removes a shaving's thickness – typically 2 thousandths of an inch ($\frac{1}{20}$mm) from the surface, creating a temporary step in the wood under the mouth. This results in more pressure under the sole in front of the mouth than behind it, which is

helpful because the pressure stops fibres peeling up ahead of the blade. If the mouth is set too wide, the grain will already be torn by the time the cutter reaches it. Setting the mouth very narrow minimizes tearing, but it can also cause the plane to choke up with shavings. The ideal mouth width has to be a compromise, depending on the nature of the wood and the fineness of shavings.

BAILEY OR NORRIS?

The cutter must be set so it just emerges from the plane's mouth. Traditionally, the depth of cut was adjusted with a hammer, knocking the back of the

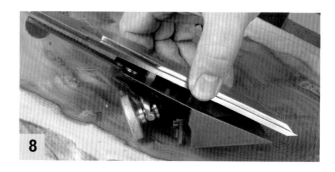

8

9

7 Planing against the grain, fibres are prized out of the wood and peel ahead of the cutting edge.

8 A bailey adjuster has a thumbwheel behind the frog and lateral adjustment lever above it.

9 This plane uses a variation on the Norris adjuster mechanism with combined depth and lateral adjustor above the frog.

JARGON BUSTING

Bedrock planes – this is a version of a Bailey hand plane with improved frog fixings.

blade for a deeper cut and the back of the plane for a shallower one. A Victorian tool designer, Leonard Bailey, introduced a thumbwheel adjustor screw behind the frog to move a lever passing through a hole in the chip-breaker and extend or withdraw the cutter. A separate 'lateral' lever engages in a slot in the blade for sideways adjustment. The Norris adjustor combines both depth and lateral functions in a single pivoted thumbwheel screw above the blade. Either type of adjustor needs to be lightly wound clockwise, to take up any backlash in the mechanism, before the plane is to be used.

BLOCK PLANES

The bench planes that have been considered so far have the bevelled side of the cutter laid against a frog, normally at 45°. Block planes, sometimes known as 'bevel-up planes', have the cutter the other way up with the flat side laid down against the ramped body of the plane.

The shallow angle of this ramp may be as low as 12°, so it might look as if the block plane slices at a lower angle. However, with a cutter bevel ground at 30°, the angle between its upper surface and the sole would be 42°, so it is not much different from a normal bench plane. Instead of using a frog to shift the cutter forward in the mouth, block planes have a sliding front on the sole, allowing the mouth front to be moved towards the cutter. The main advantage of block planes is their pure simplicity and their low profile making them stable and allowing small ones to fit easily in one hand. This makes them ideal for edge-trimming jobs.

10 Bolts securing the bailey frog are inaccessible beneath the irons.

11 The Bedrock frog is firmly secured by dowel pins, conveniently clamped from behind.

12 Small block planes fit comfortably in one hand and are perfect for doing fine work.

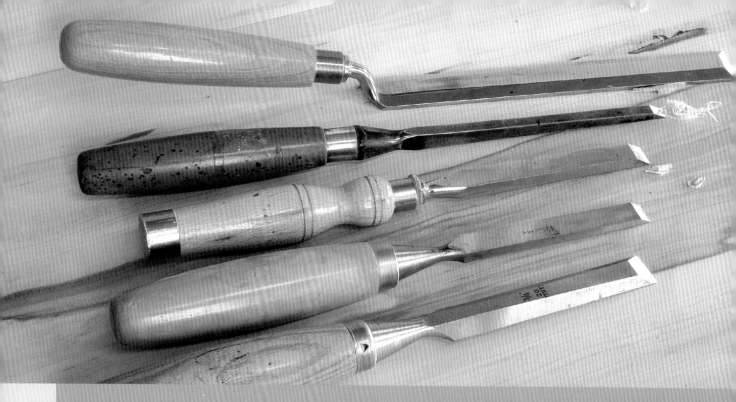

Chisels

Chisels work like wedges, driven between the chippings they are removing and the wood you need to leave behind. They come into their own for making hand-cut joints as well as for squaring up edges or sockets left rounded or ragged by machines.

There are two main chiselling actions – chopping and paring. Chopping is cutting into the depth of the wood, usually through the grain fibres, which often involves striking the chisel's handle with a mallet. Chisels designed for chopping are short and sturdy, sometimes with metal ferrules to prevent the wooden handle splitting. Paring is chiselling a thin sliver off the wood by hand force using a slicing action, often along the grain but sometimes across it. Chisels designed for paring are long and slender.

JARGON BUSTING

Ferrule – a metal hoop or ring around a wooden chisel handle to prevent it splitting.

ABOVE Chisels, from top to bottom: cranked paring chisel, registered mortice chisel, mortice chisel, firmer chisel, bevel-edged chisel.

CHISEL TYPES

Bevel-edged chisels are similar in shape to the type often sold for general-purpose joinery but slimmer. Long-handled versions provide finer control and are particularly suitable for paring flat, straight edges. A crank in the shaft of some paring chisels allows the underside to be laid flat on a surface and used like a bull-nosed plane in tight corners. The main advantage of a bevel-edge is that the tip can access tight crannies, like the corners of dovetail sockets, but the limitation is that the narrow sides will not locate the end squarely in a socket.

Firmer chisels are designed for chopping but can also be used for paring. The blade has a rectangular cross-section for maximum strength and to keep it square in a recess. If the handle is wooden and designed for striking, it will have a ferrule or metal ring on top to stop it splitting and a leather washer between the handle and the hilt of the blade to soften the blow. This design is known as a mortice chisel, because one of its main purposes is for chopping out mortices. Some mortice chisels have deep sides, helping them locate or register in the slot they are opening up, hence these are called registered mortice chisels.

JAPANESE CHISELS

Japanese chisels have become very popular with Western makers over recent years. They are made with laminated blades, the underside being hard steel, forged on to an upper and shaft made from soft iron. One of the first things you may notice is that the undersides of Japanese chisels have a hollow-ground scoop ground into them rather than being flat. The idea is to make flattening of the land around the edge easier but it can also make the chisels harder to guide when paring a flat surface.

There are a great many variations in design, one of the most common being the stumpy little butt chisels called Oire Nomi. These have a short bevel-edged blade and come in a range of widths between ⅛in and 1⅝in (3mm and 42mm). The steel hoop on top of the oak handle is designed to be tapped with a metal mallet. This makes them great for chopping joints but they are intended for use on softwoods, so you need to resist the temptation to hit them too hard which will chip the cutting edge.

It may be surprising that incredibly fine control can be achieved with a long paring chisel such as Shinogi Usu Tsuki Nomi. This big tool is reserved for the fine work, because with the long handle gripped near the end, the other hand can direct the blade with small movements.

1 Japanese chisels have a large hollow area ground out of the flat underside.

2 Iron and steel laminations clearly visible above the microbevel.

3 Paring a dovetail socket with a fine Japanese chisel.

CHOPPING WITH CHISELS

Chisels tend to wander while you are chopping. A light tap to mark the place followed by a firmer blow to make the cut will help avoid this. If you are chopping back to a line, make the last cut very thin to avoid the chisel being forced back beyond the line. With dovetails, for example, you would remove the bulk of the material with a saw and finally chop up to the line with the chisel.

A wooden mallet applied with light, controlled strokes is unlikely to harm a wooden or plastic chisel handle. However, if you are going to use a metal mallet or a very hard wooden one such as lignum vitae on a wooden handled chisel, make sure it has a ferruled top.

Chopping with a mallet and chisel is the traditional way to cut mortices. A succession of shallow chops is made along the length of the mortice to remove a layer of chippings. This is pared out ready for the next layer. Produce the cleanest cuts with the least strokes by chopping

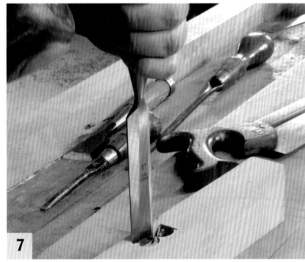

4 Chopping a through mortice joint in the arm of a chair with a mortice chisel.

5 Chop out a sucession of short-grained chips.

6 The chisel is chosen to match the socket width.

7 Squaring up a mortice after using a pillar drill.

mortices to the same width as your most suitable chisel. Furniture-makers rarely mortice this way nowadays unless for a special joint. Much more commonly, they use a hollow chisel morticer, a slot morticer or a domino jointer. Alternatively they remove the bulk of the waste with a drill or router and chop with a chisel to square up the ends.

PARING WITH CHISELS

Cutting the wood using a slicing action or paring with a chisel is very much a two-handed operation. It is essential that the wood is securely clamped before you try paring it because if it flies loose the chisel blade can shoot forwards, possibly causing damage or injury.

Paring chisels have bevel edges to allow them into tight recesses. The handles are usually rounded to allow a tight grip. As you pare along the wood, the flat underside of the blade guides the chisel

edge and keeps it travelling in a straight line, without digging in or hopping out. If you are paring a wide cut you can improve your control by making a succession of cuts side by side, using a wide chisel. One side of the blade glides across the surface produced by the previous cuts while the edge on the other side does the cutting on each new stroke. For fine paring, one hand grips the handle to drive it forward while the other holds the shaft to restrain the movement.

8 Wood is securely clamped before paring.

8

9

The sharp edge of the paring chisel needs to be in gentle contact with the wood before any force is applied. Apply force to the handle with your dominant hand while the other hand pinches the flat upper and lower side of the blade and guides it across the wood.

Paring can be horizontal with the chisel handle gripped like a knife, or vertical with the handle gripped like a dagger. If the chisel starts to judder, angle the blade slightly to alternate sides so it cuts across the ripples left by the previous cut. Make a succession of cuts to avoid paring too deep so the force is kept light and you keep the tool in control. All movements must be slow and deliberate – you want no surprises when chiselling. If you need to pare right along the edge of end grain, work inwards from both sides to prevent the tool flying off the far end of the cut and splitting the wood as it goes.

9 Paring the inside of a chamfered joint.

10 Paring a chamfer using the bevel of the chisel as a reference surface.

10

SHARPENING

Chisels must have razor-sharp edges for furniture-making. When you buy a moderately priced new chisel, it will probably be sold with an inadequate cutting edge, suitable for joinery but not for fine work. Some high-specification chisels are sold with well-prepared edges, but even these will need some honing or grinding before long. Sharp chisels are safer because there is no need to force them, so they give you full control. A poorly ground chisel edge leads to scars of the struggle on the finished project whereas the less force you need to apply, the less damage can be done to the wood.

Before you use a chisel for the first time, flatten and polish the back of it on a flat waterstone or diamond whetstone. It is important not to let the handle ride up while grinding as this would round the underside of the chisel, preventing it from cutting straight. It is normal to use a medium-coarse stone grade of about 800 first to do the flattening, then polish with a fine stone of 4000 grade or higher to create a dull mirror finish. The idea is to flatten and polish the end of the back $\frac{3}{8}$–$\frac{5}{8}$in (10–15mm) from the cutting edge. This may take quite a few minutes, with firm finger pressure on the end.

If the front of the blade is in reasonable shape, grind the chisel at a slightly steeper angle than the main slope, to make a secondary bevel on the tip. This will form a narrow band, and you can grind or hone it on a fine stone very quickly. Some furniture-makers take pride in doing this by hand and eye, but for a reliable precise result a honing guide makes more sense.

Makers will often hollow-grind chisels on a waterstone wheel. This allows the secondary bevel to be given a shallow angle on fine-paring chisels. Hollow grinding is repeated very infrequently because you can re-grind the flat secondary bevel using a honing guide on a flat stone many times before re-visiting the wheel.

Any chisel edge will dull with use, especially if you are chopping deep into hardwoods with a high mineral content like teak or elm. The compromise between working with a blunt edge and spending too much time at the grindstone is something you need to judge – for example, a fine-paring chisel kept for delicate work is less tolerant of a dull edge than a firmer chisel.

11

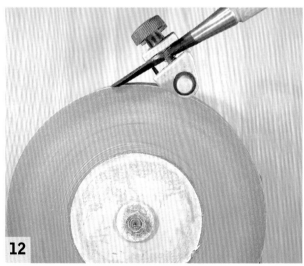

12

11 The honing guide holds the chisel at a fixed angle to the stone.

12 Grinding the main bevel on a butt chisel.

Saws

Sawing by hand may look old fashioned but, with some practice, it is the best way for furniture-makers to cut exactly where and how they need, especially while they produce fine joints and details.

In the past, makers would have owned a vast range of crosscut saws, rip-saws (used for cutting along a board), panel saws and back saws, with various sizes of each. They all would be optimized for specific tasks and designed to make the hard labour of sizing and shaping timber as efficient as possible.

Nowadays, furniture-makers are more likely to use fixed machines for large or repetitive sawing tasks. However, a sawbench is not an investment to rush into – it can come later. Handheld power saws can be useful for rough preparation tasks, but their lack of fine control and coarse finish means that furniture-makers regard them more as DIY equipment. A better way to start is to pay a timber yard to do the basic work of machine sawing and to focus your attention on the fine skill of hand sawing.

ABOVE The saw cut or kerf follows closely against the side of the knife mark.

MARKING OUT

Skilful sawing involves following a line marked on the timber, and the finer that the line is, the more precisely you will be able to follow it. An ordinary pencil has graphite $\frac{1}{16}$in (2mm) thick on which a pencil sharpener can produce a fine conical point. Unfortunately, the point rapidly becomes blunt on wood and the line tapers to a fat smudge.

Sharpening with a knife can produce a fine chisel-shaped end on the graphite that lasts better because it has a wider tip. The lines are just as fine, providing you keep the tip edgewise to the line direction. Sharpen pencils with your fingers gripping away from the knife to avoid accidents and hone up the tip on fine glass paper. However, you cannot accurately tell exactly how wide the pencil line will be, so I suggest that you do not use pencils for marking critical dimensions, only for doing rough positioning.

Propelling pencils hold fine graphite – typically $\frac{1}{32}$in (0.5mm), with the advantage that their lines do not change in thickness as the tip wears down. The knowledge that your line is a constant $\frac{1}{32}$in (0.5mm) wide will give you the chance to use it accurately. Whether you cut to one side of it or the other or split it down the middle, you take control of the process.

KNIFE LINES

Knife lines can be much finer. If the blade is sharp and ground to an acute angle, lines of about 4 thousandths of an inch (0.1mm) should be quite visible. Of course, that does not mean that the mark is necessarily accurate, it depends on the shape of the knife and how you use it.

Marking knives are normally flat on one side and bevel ground on the other. That includes European-style knives with wooden handles and the Japanese types, which are a strip of bare laminated steel. The idea is that you hold the blade vertically and run the flat side against an edge so the cutting tip is directly beneath the edge. For marking in confined spaces – such as when making hand-cut dovetail joints – a scalpel fitted with No. 11 blades can be very effective. You can make knife lines easier to see afterwards by rubbing over them with a soft pencil, then abrasive paper, leaving the groove clearly emphasized in black.

1 A chisel-ended pencil leaves the finest line, while the propelling pencil line has constant width.

2 Knife lines are much finer than pencil and can be more accurately placed.

DIRECT MARKING

Each time you take a measurement, however careful it may be, there will be some inaccuracy or error. This is inevitable because the ruler only has a limited number of graduations and our eyes can only see the ruler and the marking line with limited accuracy.

This means if you measure the width of a joint, then measure again to mark the other side of the joint, the errors will add together. To avoid this, furniture-makers try to mark pieces directly off one another whenever possible. Another advantage of direct marking, rather than measuring, is that it does not clutter the brain up with numbers and helps you concentrate on the layout.

BACK SAWS

Saws for ripping and crosscutting may be 600mm (24in) long or more, while saws for making small, accurate cuts are typically half this length. They have a heavy gauge metal back along the top edge. This has the dual purpose of stiffening the blade and applying weight over the teeth so you do not need to press down with the handle. The general name for this type is a 'back saw', but they are more commonly called tenon saws because they are used for cutting the shoulders and cheeks of tenon joints. Tenon saw teeth have a pitch of about 5⁄64in (2mm) between points (12tpi), which is twice as fine as a large handsaw designed for ripping. A shorter variety of back saw, which is normally 8in (200mm) or less, is the dovetail saw. The blade is also thinner and narrower and the teeth are finer than a tenon saws, typically having a pitch of 20tpi (1.2mm). Because the metal parts are smaller, some tool designers have also tried to make the wooden handles on dovetail saws smaller, so the saw will feel balanced to hold.

When the handle has the lower part cut away (so a large hand can still hold it), the style is known as a pistol grip. The teeth on a ripsaw have steep angled fronts filed to a straight edge to chisel along the fibres of wood, while crosscut saw teeth are more laid-back but filed to points so they sever the grain without tearing in. Panel saws are a general-purpose compromise and follow the crosscut pattern, which is more forgiving, but slower.

Dovetail saws used to be made with crosscut teeth, but recognizing that most of the cuts in joints are along the grain, they are now commonly made with ripsaw teeth. Looking at a sawblade edgeways, you will see that the teeth are 'set', or bent slightly outwards to alternate sides. This makes the sawcut, or kerf, a little wider than the blade so it will move freely in it and not jam. It also allows the blade to wiggle around a bit in the kerf, which is a mixed blessing – the advantage is it allows you to straighten up the blade if it starts to go off course, but the downside is that it allows it to go off course in the first place. People often find a wide kerf is helpful at first in letting them straighten the cut, but with more experience they start to correct subconsciously for straightness, which means the saw never gets a chance to go off course. Then, having too much set is an irritation as it produces a jumpy blade and a wiggly kerf.

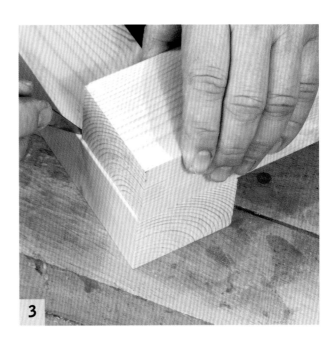

3

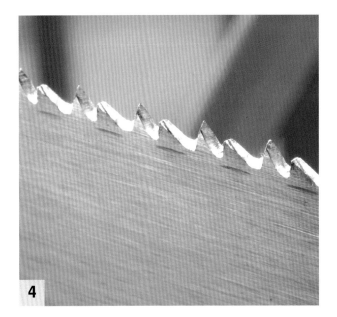

3 Directly marking one piece off another eliminates measurement errors.

4 Saw teeth are set on alternate sides so the blade will not jam in its kerf.

5 A panel saw cuts deeper than a back saw.

6 Dovetail saws are the finest type of back saw a furniture-maker uses.

JARGON BUSTING

kerf – the slot left by a saw blade.
tpi – teeth per inch.

HAND-SAW BLADES

Quality saws used by furniture-makers have blades made from high-grade alloy spring steel so the user can adjust the set, or re-sharpen them by using a triangular Swiss file or send them to be tuned by a 'saw-doctor'. General-purpose saws for DIY jobs and coarse woodworking have hardened teeth, known as hardpoints. These are shaped to give a fast cut but not a fine one. After shaping and sharpening, the teeth on these saws are heat-treated in a high-frequency electric induction process in order to harden them. It is quite easy to spot if a saw is a hardpoint because the teeth are blue/black coloured. A hardpoint saw cannot be re-sharpened, nor is it possible to adjust the set of the teeth, as they would snap off, weakened by bending. You must replace it when the performance drops, making it less suitable for fine furniture work.

FINE SAWING

For fine sawing, clamp the timber low down in a vice so that it does not vibrate, and arrange it so the cut will be truly vertical. Grip the saw handle with three fingers and a thumb, the index finger being laid alongside the handle, pointing along the

7 A triangular file is used to sharpen the teeth.

8 The set is restored on each tooth ready for sharpening.

9 Three-finger grip on the handle with the index finger pointing along the back of the saw.

direction of the blade to help lock the wrist. At the start of a cut, the hand not holding the saw grips the timber, with the thumbnail used as a guide against the smooth part of the sawblade.

The first pull-stroke should not dig in or jump but just mark the surface of the wood, ready for the first action stroke when the saw is pushed – if you are using a Japanese saw then swap pull for push. With the kerf established, the upper arm hangs vertically from the shoulder while the forearm moves too and fro like a piston, keeping the blade exactly vertical and applying very little downward pressure.

KEEPING IN LINE

Once a saw kerf has started to wander off the line, it can be very difficult to get on again. It is far better if you can prevent it drifting in the first place. Attention is needed to keep the teeth on track running down one edge of the line – if you concentrate on every stroke, the blade should never get a chance to wander off course, and you will never be faced with the near impossible task of getting back into line again. With practice, this becomes a good habit. Keep your nose centred over the saw so you can view both sides of the saw-blade for improved accuracy on fine cuts. When it comes to joints, saw on the inside edge of the line when removing waste from a socket and from the outside when sawing a pin.

10 It is preferable to angle the workpiece and keep the saw vertical.

11 A bench hook, simply made from three pieces of timber, helps accurate crosscuts.

12 A diagonal grip in the vice allows you to watch the cut follow lines on both surfaces.

13 Saw on the inside edge of the line when removing waste from a socket.

14 Kerfs from: 1) modern hardpoint back saw, 2) traditional Sheffield tenon saw, 3) Japanese dokuzi saw with hardpoint teeth and 4) a carefully adjusted English dovetail saw.

TECHNICAL TIP

If you find your 'straight' saw cuts are not always straight, it could be the saw. Sight along the blade to check it is not bent. More often though, people find the problem is to do with the way the saw is used and that means a bit more practice is required. You can then cut accurate, good-looking joints that will do justice to your projects.

Cabinet scrapers

A scraper may sound like the sort of crude tool you would use when preparing for decorating but is actually an invaluable addition to the cabinetmaker's toolbox that removes fine shavings – leaving crisp professional-looking surfaces and edges.

The basic cabinetmaker's scraper, which is just a flat piece of steel, could not be simpler. However, if it is properly prepared and sharpened, you can use it with the lightest touch to produce a fine finish regardless of grain direction. You can also use it for coarse jobs like removing glue lines from the surface of joints. A scraper has other advantages over abrasives such as sandpaper or steel wool. It removes shavings rather than dust so it does not contaminate one

ABOVE The scraper produces fine shavings, removing the torn-out grain left by the plane.

wood with the dust from the other. The shavings do not clog up the pores of open-grained woods such as oak, which some abrasives will do. More sophisticated types of scraper are useful for dealing with larger surfaces or shaped edges.

PREPARING A SCRAPER

Cabinet scrapers need a few minutes' preparation as the edge supplied by the manufacturer will be the wrong shape and too rough for immediate use. The idea is first to produce a clean right-angled arris where the flat faces meet the straight edges. The edges are then curled over to produce a

JARGON BUSTING

burnisher – a tool that is a steel rod used to flatten scraper edges.

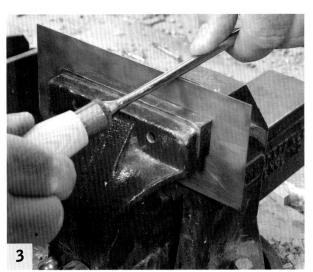

microscopic hook suitable for scraping. With a normal straight scraper blade, you do this four times by preparing both sides of each long edge to give you four working edges.

Start by flattening both the faces of the scraper blade on a medium-coarse grade stone. You could use carborundum (silicon carbide) or diamond lapping plates – but avoid adding oil for it will contaminate the blade's surface. I use a waterstone to eliminate the risk of getting oil stains on my furniture. Beware that any water left on the scraper will produce rust and pitting, making it harder to prepare next time. Keep a towel handy to dry it and avoid damage. Concentrate on smoothing the faces around each edge of the blade; the middle does not matter. Once you have produced an even, grey dullness right along the edge, turn the scraper around and prepare the other three long edges.

Now you need to flatten the edges. A scraper blade is typically about $\frac{1}{25}$in (1mm) thick so standing it on edge is no mean feat. In fact it is nearly impossible to hold it at a fixed 90° by hand. However, if you hold the blade with one hand at each end and spring it into an arc, the bowed edge will rest at right angles on the stone while you work it up and down to true the edge. Then repeat the flattening and edge preparation using a fine stone, then look closely, preferably using a magnifying glass, to check there are no pits, jagged points or wire edges on the blade.

HOOKED EDGE SCRAPER

The hook, which will do all the scraping work, is formed by rubbing the edges of the blade with a burnisher. You can buy burnishers for scraper blades

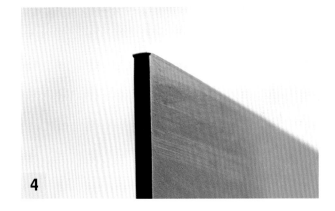

but, being rather specialized, they often cost more than the scrapers themselves. Another tool that will do the job equally well is a screwdriver, provided the shaft is made from hard steel and is not plated.

1 Polish the scraper blade on a stone.

2 Burnish each edge of the face to compress steel into a lip.

3 Burnish the edge to turn the lip into a hooked burr.

4 Close-up of the burr formed on each side of the scraper.

Lay the scraper blade flat on a wooden surface and, holding the burnisher shaft at an angle of about 10° to the scraper face, rub it along the edge, pressing firmly. The idea of this is to produce a lip on the edge of the scraper blade by forcing metal out from the edge of the surface. Depending on whether you want to make a fine scraper or a coarse one, repeat this action twice or many times.

Next, turn the scraper blade on edge and clamp it in a vice. Once again, using the shaft of the burnisher, press firmly down, this time on the edge of the blade, and stroke along the length of each long edge. This action will draw the steel into a hook on the edge of the face of the scraper blade. Again, repeat a number of strokes for a coarse scraper or just one or two for a fine one.

SCRAPING SURFACES

Having prepared four good hooked edges on the scraper blade, it is time to apply them to the wood. Using both hands, grip both ends of the blade, fingers in front and thumbs behind. Press with the thumbs and bend the blade in an arc while tilting it forwards on the wooden surface. Press lightly on the wood and slide the blade forward to remove the slightest of shavings. Shavings should be thin enough to read through, but should not turn to dust. If the blade digs in then the hook is probably too large. If you can only produce dust, then the hook is probably too small.

Experiment by varying the pressure and the angle at which you hold the blade. Try all four edges and see if some are better than others. A small hook can be increased by more strokes with the burnisher. However, if the hook is too large or misshapen, I am afraid it is back to the grindstone to start again.

Once you have a working scraper blade you will find it produces a pit-free surface on any timber at any angle to the grain. With practice, you can tell by the feel and sound whether the scraper is working properly. There should not be any judder and, because the shavings removed are so fine, there will be little resistance even from the hardest woods.

SCRAPING LARGER AREAS

The cabinet scraper produces a lot of friction when it is cutting and, being only a thin piece of metal, the resulting heat has nowhere to go. Because of this, the temperature rises quickly when you work on large surfaces and the result can be burned thumbs.

Devices for holding a scraper blade have been around for a century or more, and their use makes very good sense if, for example, you are smoothing a table top. This is a common task for a scraper because table tops are nearly always made from a succession of boards glued together side by side. In removing the glue line where the boards meet you will probably encounter conflicting wood grain directions. A scraper used for the whole table top will flatten it superbly without the risk of bumps and hollows that a sander can produce.

5 Scraping inlays of contrasting woods.

6 The Stanley No.80 (left) looks like a spokeshave – but it is a scraper. A Lie Nielsen 112 scraper (right).

Other scraper holder designs look more like short, wide planes with handles to the front and rear. Models like the 212 and 112, originally designed by Stanley and now made by Lie Nielsen and others, have variable-angle clamps to hold the blade. This makes them versatile for dealing with timbers with the most awkward interlocking grain.

To set the height of the blade on a scraper plane, stand it on a completely flat surface; a piece of glass or a granite tile is better than wood for this. Release the blade and lower it so that it touches the surface evenly from side to side. Now you know the blade tip is level with the sole, you can fine-adjust the depth of cut with the angle-adjuster screws.

The Stanley No. 80 is a scraper holder designed for this type of task. The blade is made thicker than a handheld scraper blade because it is mechanically pressed into a curve with a thumbscrew. The thickness reduces heating effects and makes it less prone to chatter. The No. 80 is held by a pair of gull-wing-style handles, one on each side, which make it look like an outsized spokeshave.

MAKING A SCRATCH STOCK

A simple tool to make and use, the scratch stock is excellent for shaping edges or making grooves to take fine inlays. You can buy them, but equally effective is an old marker gauge with the pin removed and a slot sawn in the stem. File the profile of the shape you want on the edge of a strip of tool steel, made from a discarded sawblade. Slide the steel into the slot in the gauge's stem. Arrange the small cutting edges of the steel to protrude from the side then pinch it in place with the thumbscrew in the stock. To use the scratch stock, slide it repeatedly along the edge to be shaped. Work it in both directions or whichever way gives the smoother result.

SHAPED BLADES

Shaped scraper blades are sold for work on curved wooden surfaces. One of the commonest is the gooseneck scraper, which will cope with a variety of inside and outside curves. These are prepared in the same way as the rectangular scraper, although you will need to use slip stones to smooth inside curved scraper blade edges.

Edge joints

The trouble with trees is they do not make wide enough wood for a lot of furniture projects. Combined with the amount wasted converting them into boards, this means that wide surfaces nearly always need to be made from edge-jointed timber.

Making one of the hardwood chopping boards shown here is a good exercise in the essential task of planing hardwood to a flat surface with an even thickness and square edges, and then jointing boards, edge-to-edge to make a useful width.

LAYOUT & SAWING

Beech (*Fagus sylvatica*) or sycamore (*Acer pseudoplatanus*) are both suitable native woods for a chopping board as they will not taint or poison food, in the way that yew (*Taxus baccata*) or some tropical woods might. To make a chopping board like the one in the following pictures you will need to buy timber approximately 1¼in (30mm) thick by 6in (150mm) wide, cut to 30in (800mm) in length.

ABOVE Using varied woods, like sycamore and walnut, makes a feature of the edge joints in this chopping board.

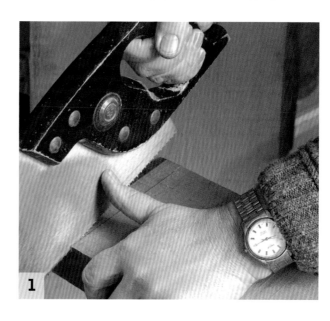

1

The first stage is to saw off two pieces of timber, each equal to the board length of 15in (400mm). The ends will be trued up with a plane after gluing. It is very important that the cut is just outside the line and that splits in the dried ends of the timber are removed.

REFERENCE FACE

The plane used needs to be fairly long with a straight enough sole to create a truly flat edge on the timber – one that is flat within less than a shaving's thickness. Squinting across the board while turning it, allows you to see if it is cupped, bowed or twisted and to judge which face is best. It is sometimes advantageous with difficult grain to angle the plane to the direction of movement so it cuts on the skew. This has several beneficial effects. Primarily, it gives the cutter a slicing action, able to sever fibres, rather than lift them. It also reduces the effective width of the cutting edge, reducing drag.

Initially, the shavings will spit out as short, scrappy pieces as the plane skims over humps and bumps. Patience is needed at this stage – it is tempting to set the cutter a little deeper which is fine unless it starts to tear the surface, in which case it will require more planing to remove. Start each stroke with more pressure on the front knob of the plane and the cutter short of the wood. Try to keep your arms rigid while using your legs to move your body and the plane through the stroke. Finish with more pressure applied to the rear tote of the plane and the cutter off the far edge of the wood. Once you have achieved a flat surface, long silky shavings will emerge from the plane. The cutter can be adjusted finely so the shavings are thin enough to read through. A succession of straight passes across the whole surface with a slight overlap should produce a full-length fine shaving. This proves there are no dips that would cause a break in the shaving.

1 Saw the board into equal-length pieces.

2 Planing the rough surface produces short, scrappy shavings.

3 Once the surface is smooth, shavings emerge long and silky.

WINDING STICKS

A good way of checking if there is a twist in the boards is to use a pair of straight square section rods called winding sticks. One stick is laid on each end of the board so they adopt the angle of the surface at the ends. Sighting across the near stick to look at the far one, you raise and lower your head, noting when the far stick is just hidden from view. At this instant, both sides should disappear simultaneously; otherwise, the surface is 'in wind' or twisted. Alternatively, with small pieces of wood you may find that by sighting carefully along the board, you can see the far end of the board disappear as you lower your head in the same way, but without the aid of winding sticks.

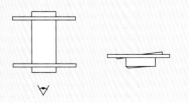

SQUARES

An accurate square is an essential tool for many woodworking tasks. You may wish to choose a woodworker's try square with a rosewood or ebony stock, or the less handsome but more precise engineer's square with a steel stock. The try square you use must be accurate and you can check this against another square of already known quality. Alternatively, press the stock against a straight-edged piece of scrap. Mark a line against the blade of the square running across the scrap. Now flip the stock over, press it against the straightedge again and slide the blade up against the original line. If it lines up accurately, then the square is true.

REFERENCE EDGE

Check the edge of a board by pressing the stock of a square against the reference face while holding it up with a light behind. If you can see a glimmer between the blade of the square and the edge of the timber, then the edge is not at right angles to the face. Try this at several positions along the edge, which may have a twist in it.

While edge-planing the timber, it may be stood on edge against a bench stop or else clamped in a vice. During this task, the front of the plane, rather than being grasped by the knob, is pinched between the thumb above the body and the fingers

JARGON BUSTING

try square – an L-shaped tool for checking right angles.

4 Check the edge with an accurate square.

5 Planing the edge with the fingers as a guide fence.

6 The reference face and the reference edges are marked.

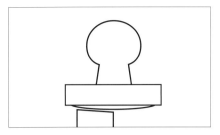

The cutter has a slight curve ground on its front edge.

beneath the sole, just ahead of the mouth. This then allows the fingers to act as guides, closely controlling the position of the cutter just above the timber's edge. If the cutter has a slight curve ground on its front edge, then moving the centre line of the plane to one side will cut more deeply on that side, allowing you to control the angle of the surface and then level it as required by the square (as shown in this drawing). For the final pass, the plane is centred on the edge, producing a long, continuous fine shaving with no breaks that would indicate dips are present.

Whenever we make a measurement or mark on wood for planing or cutting, there will be a slight error in this, though hopefully a very small one. The reference face and the reference edge are given pencil marks, so you can remember which they are, once the others are planed. The idea is that if you always make measurements against the same face and edge, an accumulation of errors will not build up.

THICKNESSING

To mark the thickness of the wood you will need to gauge a line all around the edge at a constant distance from the reference face. The instrument used for doing this is called a marking gauge. Traditionally, this consists of a wooden stock that slides up and down a wooden stem and can be locked in position with a thumbscrew. The stem either has a pin projecting from one side or a small blade, in which case it is called a cutting gauge.

7 Gauge the thickness with a line all around.

8 The opposite face is planed to the line for a uniform thickness.

While the cutting gauge is somewhat easier to use, both these traditional tools have a reputation for being awkward. They tend to get caught in the wood fibres so the lines they mark can be jagged. Several newer makes of marking gauge use a sharp-edged steel disc on the end of a metal stem. This type of gauge still needs careful use to apply firm pressure between the stock and the reference face, while pressing the cutting disc lightly into the wood. However, it is a considerable improvement as it does not judder on long edges and it allows the wheel to be rolled across short ones. With the thickness lines marked, the opposite face and edge are planed in the same manner, but this time working carefully down to the line.

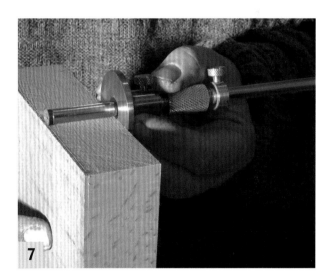

7

8

JOINTING

Having prepared two or more pieces of timber of the same length and thickness, the edges can be glued together to make a multiple-width board. It is most important the surfaces end up level with one another and that there is no gap in the joint that would cause weakness.

Clamp the pieces face-to-face in the vice so both pieces have grain running along the edge in the same direction. By planing the pair together, you can ensure that, even if they are not perfectly at right angles to the faces, any offset in the angles will cancel out when the edges are pressed together.

9 For jointing, both edges are clamped face-to-face and planed together.

10 A desk light reveals any gaps between the edges.

This may not be obvious but it becomes clearer when you try it. When you believe they are planed straight and true, unclamp and place one edge on top of the other with a bright light behind. The truth is revealed by any glimmer of light you see through gaps between them.

If the wood was originally flat-sawn by the timber converter – as opposed to quarter-sawn – there will be annual growth rings visible as arcs across the end grain. Further drying of the wood causes each board to cup slightly, but you can cancel out the overall effect across a jointed board if you arrange the arcs to alternate in direction.

GLUING UP

Most woodworking tasks can be taken slowly with plenty of time for thought and checking along the way. The exception to this is the glue-up which is best described as organized panic – organized, that is, if you plan ahead by adjusting cramps and checking they hold the timber pieces level and true before applying any glue. Use PVA glue and apply it evenly to one edge using a brush to spread it. Bring the two pieces together with the faces aligned as accurately as you can. Apply moderate pressure with the cramps, which may cause small beads of glue to ooze out. Any more would indicate you have been too generous with it. Do not distort the cramps by applying excess pressure, as this will result in a warped joint. After the glue has set for

11

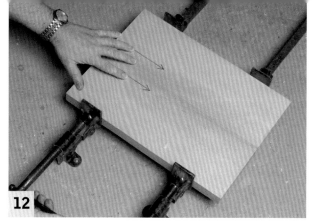

12

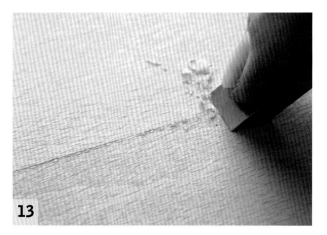

13

14

at least as long as the manufacturer recommends, preferably longer such as overnight in cool conditions, the cramps are released and hardened beads of excess glue chiselled off the surface. The jointed board is then planed in a succession of overlapping passes, checking for flatness, as before.

END GRAIN AND CHAMFERS

There is an approach to furniture-making, often associated with the Arts and Crafts style, that tends to chamfer all the external sharp edges or 'arrises' with a narrow 45° plane cut. This is not only a

11 Water-resistant glue is brushed evenly along one edge.

12 Rigid T-bar sash-cramps hold the edges together while the glue sets.

13 Beads of excess glue are chipped off.

14 The full-width surface is planed in a succession of overlapping passes.

15 Chamfered edges protect the end grain, which planes in complete shavings – joint and all.

styling feature, it is a way of ensuring that hand-planed edges do not splinter, especially when planing end grain. If the chamfers are cut first, then planing along end grain is no more difficult than planing along an edge, providing the cutter is sharp and adjusted for fine shaving to avoid judder.

If you want to plane the end grain straight from edge to edge without leaving chamfers, it is quite essential to only plane onto the wood but not to plane off the far edge. Next approach the wood from the other edge doing the same thing.

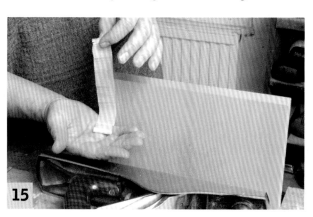

15

Carcass joints

Cabinetmakers will really benefit from learning and practising a good selection of carcass joints. Here we get to grips with the hugely versatile mortice and tenon joint and some of its common variations.

Frame and panel construction is a well-proven technique for making up solid-wood furniture carcasses that are sturdy, efficient in their use of materials and resistant to wood movement with changes in air humidity. The frames consist of vertical corner posts, or stiles, with horizontal rails between them, sometimes divided by muntins or intermediate vertical rails. The main device for joining frames is the mortice and tenon joint.

There are many variants of mortice and tenon so here we will look at three of them – the simple bridle joint, the stronger haunched mortice and tenon and also the through mortice and tenon, which can be held in place with a wedge. Other carcass joints included are the halving joint where a rail crosses a muntin and the carcass dovetail

ABOVE A carcass dovetail front rail and a haunched tenon side rail.

joint, which provides the best solution for a corner needing some additional strength, such as a top rail fixed into a stile.

JARGON BUSTING

mortice – hole to receive a tenon and form a joint, usually rectangular.
tenon – peg to be pressed into a mortice to form a joint.
haunch – an extra part on tenon shoulder to prevent twisting.

BRIDLE JOINTS

The bridle joint or slot joint is the simplest mortice and tenon. The mortice of the bridle joint is an open-sided slot in the end of one piece of wood, while the tenon takes the form of a pin, which is the full width of the timber, reduced in thickness, allowing the two parts to join as an L-shape. It can be used for small frames like cupboard doors although it does not have the strength of a joint where the tenon is fully surrounded by the mortice.

A mortice gauge is a handy variant of the marking gauge with dual marking points. This allows you to adjust the distance between the points to fix the width of the joint, ideally matching the width of a suitable chisel. With the width set, the stock on the gauge can be slid up and down the stem to locate the joint anywhere across the depth of the timber, without changing the width of the joint. Matched pairs of markings are made with the mortice gauge on both halves of the joint. However, the shoulders, which are marked with a knife against a try square, are different.

For the pin, the shoulders run around the outside of the wood, while for the socket, there is a short shoulder mark between the gauge lines (see drawing below). The wood is clamped low in a vice, ready to be sawn using a fine tenon saw. As before, it helps if you can keep your nose above the centre of the saw and sight down each side, while

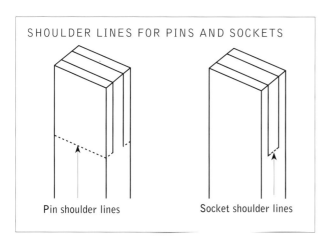

SHOULDER LINES FOR PINS AND SOCKETS

Pin shoulder lines   Socket shoulder lines

1 Points on the mortice gauge are adjusted to match the chisel width.

2 The saw follows inside the line for sockets, outside the line for pins or tenons.

3 A coping saw removes the bulk of the waste.

THE PIN OF A T-SHAPED BRIDLE JOINT

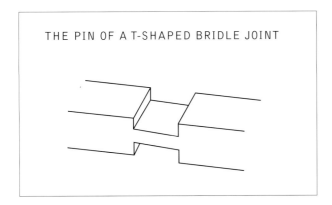

4

5

4 Shoulders sawn off leave a square tenon.

5 The bridle joint slides together.

the saw follows inside the mortice gauge line for sockets and outside of the line for pins or tenons. To remove the bulk of the waste from the socket, you can either use a coping saw or drill through the edge with a carefully aligned drill press. Either way, a thin layer of roughly cut waste should be left in the socket base for removal with a chisel.

The waste from the pins is sawn off using the bench hook for support, again keeping the kerf on the waste side of the line. Alternatively, to produce a T-shaped bridle joint, the pin can be produced partway along the timber by removing a socket from each side, like for shallow halving joints (see drawing, above left). Bridle joints should be a snug hand-push fit, but there must not be any tightness, as this would force the prongs of the socket apart.

HAUNCHED MORTICE AND TENON

The haunch is a step cut in the top of a tenon to extend its width and help prevent it from twisting in the mortice. The haunch is also useful in frame and panel work because it fills the end of the slot that holds the panel where there might otherwise be a hole. Stub mortices are blind rectangular holes, as opposed to through mortices where the tenon's end is visible on the far side.

For any right-angle jointed frame, you need to plane the timber faces flat and parallel, with both edges square to the faces. Before you cut wood to length for the rails, work out the depth of the joints and add an allowance for these. It is ideal to allow a small excess length on the corner posts or stiles as horns to be cut off once the joints are made.

The thickness of a mortice is chosen to match the width of a suitable mortice chisel. If you have a choice of mortice chisels, it is common to make the joint thickness around one-third of the thickness of the rail; that way the tenon and the wood each side of the mortice will be of similar strength. Set the distance between the two spurs on your mortice gauge to match that of the chisel width.

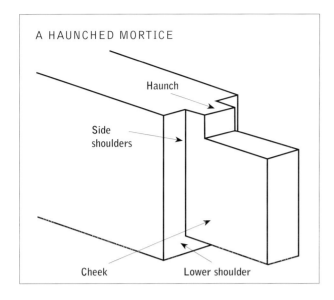

A HAUNCHED MORTICE

Haunch

Side shoulders

Cheek

Lower shoulder

6

7

8

6 Mortice and tenon widths are marked with a mortice gauge, set to match the chisel width.

7 Remove waste as a series of chippings to form a rectangular stub mortice.

8 Extend the mortice sides with a shallow kerf each side.

9 Pare out waste, forming a slot to receive the haunch.

9

TECHNICAL TIP

While you are sawing, try to position your nose centrally over the saw so you can sight down both sides of the blade at once. This enables you to see where the kerf is running in relation to the guideline and gives you maximum control.

10

11

12

The width of the haunch is normally one-third the width of the tenon, leaving two-thirds to insert into the full depth of the mortice. Mark the ends of the mortice using a try square and knife lines across the stile. Allow for a small lower shoulder on the underside of the tenon. When marking out the mortice, position the tenon about ¾in (20mm) away from the end of the timber to allow excess length for 'horns' that will be sawn off after the joint is complete. These eliminate the risk of the mortice breaking through the end of the timber during the cutting process.

The socket for a mortice can be cut entirely with a chisel. The wood must be firmly clamped down onto a flat surface using a holdfast or a G-cramp. The mortice chisel is struck with a mallet to produce a series of ⅛in (3mm) wide chippings, starting from the middle and working out towards each end of the mortice. This process is repeated until the required depth is reached. In the case of a stub tenon, the depth of the mortice would typically be two-thirds of the thickness of the stile, or less if the stile is a substantial thickness.

With the mortice chopped to full depth and the timber clamped firmly in a vice, saw a shallow kerf from each side of the mortice. The waste between

10 Saw the tenon shoulders with a kerf tight against the waste side of the line.

11 Saw waste off the tenon width in order to form the lower shoulder.

12 Mark out the depth of the haunch.

these kerfs is then chiselled out to make a slot to accommodate the haunch. The width of the tenon is marked out with the same distance between spurs on the mortice gauge so it matches the mortice. If the wood for the rail is thinner than the stile you need to readjust the stock of the gauge by sliding it along the stem so that the tenon will be central across the thickness.

Clamp the timber diagonally in the vice and saw the tenon cheeks with a kerf tight against the waste side of the line. Clamp the timber vertically and keep the saw horizontal as you saw down to the level of the tenon shoulders. With the rail laid on a bench hook or clamped horizontally in a vice, saw off waste to form the side and the lower shoulders.

The dimensions of the haunch on the tenon need to be marked directly off the mortice and adjacent slot. A small try square is useful for lining up parts while you mark out the depth and the width of the haunch. The small rectangle of waste is then sawn away to leave the required L-shaped feature on top of the tenon. Once the joint has been successfully dry-fitted, the excess length of the horns is sawn off the stile so the top is flush with the rail.

13 Mark out the width of the haunch.

14 A block of waste is sawn off the top edge of the tenon to form the haunch, then the joint can be trial fitted.

15 Excess length or 'horns' will be sawn off the stile so the top is flush with the rail.

16 Cut haunched tenons at each end of the rail.

THROUGH TENONS

Another variant of the mortice and tenon that is worth looking at is the wedged through tenon. Rather than finishing in a blind-ended socket like the stub tenon, the through tenon passes right through the mortice component. The tenon may then be sawn off flush; alternatively, it may project out of the other side. In either case, there is the opportunity to use wedges to lock the joint solidly together. Although these joints were developed centuries ago when glue was unreliable, they are attractive and extremely functional.

In the case of the flush through tenon, the wedges are hammered into prepared slots in the end of the tenon, after it has been pulled tightly through the mortice. The result is a permanently locked joint which can never be pulled apart regardless of whether it is glued.

In the case of the projected through tenon, a second mortice is chopped at right angles through the thickness of the tenon itself and a wedge is driven though this. Again, the joint is locked without glue, but this time the wedge can be easily removed again, making this an ancient design of knockdown fitting.

17 A wedged through tenon.

HALVING JOINTS

The halving joint is used where timbers cross on the same level. If you use a fine knife blade for marking and positioning the saw kerfs just inside the lines, you can make a matching pair of sockets that will fit snugly around each other. Having decided on the position of the joint, then mark the width of each piece directly off the other, to avoid the errors that would result from measurement. A try square is used to mark shoulder locations on the face and halfway across each edge. A marking gauge places a line at the depth of the socket, which is halfway through each piece of timber.

A bench hook, consisting of three pieces of softwood screwed and glued together, provides a good support for sawing shoulders on halving joints. At the very edge of each finished saw kerf the knife line will have severed the fibres, making a clean cut for what will become the inside edge of the socket. The waste can now be removed with chisels from between the kerfs. With the lower side of the timber clamped in a vice, the waste is chopped out from each side. Finally, the base of the socket is pared flat using a long-handled chisel.

Trial-fit the joint. It should go together with firm hand pressure and maybe some light persuasion with a mallet through a softwood block. Do not hammer hard – this would force the joint, distorting it, possibly splitting the wood and preventing it from separating for gluing. The joint may need adjusting by paring off its shoulders with a chisel. This can give acceptable results if done carefully but it is a time-consuming process. Alternatively, the joint may be slack and drop easily together leaving gaps. The result of either situation is that something has gone wrong with the marking or sawing. If you are satisfied with the dry-fitted joint, separate it, apply PVA glue to all the contact surfaces and press the sockets together with a clamp.

18 Marking shoulders onto the sides as far as the gauged centre line.

19 Sawing shoulders with the kerfs inside the knife lines.

20 Chopping the waste from each side.

21 Paring the base of the socket flat using a long-handled chisel.

22 The two sides of the halving joint are identical.

23 All the contact surfaces are brushed with PVA glue and the two sides pressed together with a G-cramp.

CARCASS DOVETAILS

A single dovetail is both an excellent way for joining a shallow rail into the top of a stile or post, and a good introduction to the art of dovetailing (see pages 56–67 for more variations of the dovetail joint). The convention is to use shallow angled dovetail sides of around 1:8 for hardwoods and a wider angle of around 1:6 for softwoods. You can either use a proprietary dovetail angle gauge for marking, of which there are various designs on the market, or use a sliding-bevel gauge set to the appropriate angle.

Ideally, the width of the dovetail at its narrow neck would be one-third the width of the rail. However, when the dovetail is at right angles to the haunched tenon, it may be better to reduce its width to prevent the joints meeting.

The tail is cut in a similar way to the tenon, except of course for the angles. Clamp the rail end low in the vice to prevent vibration and tilt it while cutting the dovetail sides, so the sawblade remains vertical. Saw off the shoulders as with the tenon.

Dovetail socket

Use the dovetailed end of the rail as a template for marking the dovetail socket by laying it flat on the end of the vertically clamped corner post. The best way to arrange this is to lay a plane on its side alongside the vice and clamp the post so its top is level with the upper side of the plane. Now move the plane across the bench top to act as a support and lay the dovetail so its shoulders just touch the rear face of the post. Mark around the sides and end of the tail using a fine knife or scalpel. Mark the sides of the dovetail socket at right angles to the end.

The dovetail socket waste will be mostly removed with a chisel but first saw two kerfs at angles down the sides. Clamp the post at 45° in the vice and position the saw blade so the kerf cuts into the

24 Mark sides of a dovetail against a dovetail angle gauge.

25 Tilt the timber in the vice while cutting dovetail sides so the saw remains vertical.

26

27

28

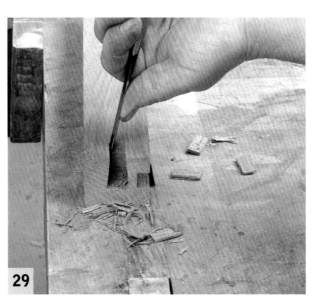

29

26 Use the dovetailed end of the rail as a template for marking the dovetail socket.

27 Saw a kerf down each side of the dovetail socket.

28 Pare and chop out waste from the dovetail socket.

29 Clean the dovetail socket corners with a fine, narrow chisel.

corner of the wood following the guide lines on both surfaces at once. This takes a bit of practice to get right, but it is easier than it sounds. Clamp the post firmly down on the bench, with a bench dog or stop behind its far end. Bevel-edged chisels are then used horizontally to pare out the waste as

a series of shavings, chopping each one off with a vertical chisel stroke at the base. Pare and chop alternately, going deeper into the wood as you form the dovetail socket. Clean the corners of the socket with a fine, narrow chisel.

Dry-fit the dovetail into its socket using firm hand pressure so there is no risk of splitting an over-tight joint. Ideally, you want to produce joints that will fit the first time without time-consuming adjustment, but until you have practised a good deal, that is a tall order. If in doubt, it is better to make the joint over-tight as this can be eased by chiselling away fine shavings later, leaving a good joint, whereas a loose-fitting or gappy joint will never be satisfactory.

Dovetails

The saying that practice makes perfect is more true of dovetailing than practically any other aspect of furniture-making. This strong and attractive joint is well worth the effort involved to get the technique right.

Dovetails have always been regarded as the furniture-maker's number one joint. They look good and they fulfil their function incredibly well – the survival of dovetail joints in heavily used furniture made centuries ago, confirms this. Furniture-makers use wide dovetail joints with several tails side by side for box and drawer construction. The main difference here is that the tails need to be smaller and finer, and the pins need shaping on each side to match the tails.

ABOVE A through dovetail joint with brown oak tails and sycamore pins.

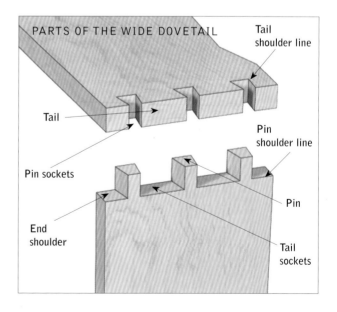

PARTS OF THE WIDE DOVETAIL

Tail shoulder line

Tail

Pin sockets

Pin shoulder line

Pin

End shoulder

Tail sockets

JARGON BUSTING

tails – fingers tapered in the side view.
pins – fingers tapered in the end view.

For fine hand-cut dovetails, it is normal to make the pins much narrower than the tails, whereas standard machine-cut pins tend to be the same width as the tails.

PREPARATION

If dovetail joints are to fit well so the finished box or drawer is straight, the timber must be flat, square edged and even thicknessed, and the ends must be cut true. Plane the face working with the grain then square the edges. Thickness both pieces, but they need not be the same thickness. It is common for the tail piece to be thinner than the pin piece. I suggest you make the tail piece no more than ½in (13mm), as this will make the joint easier to align. After sawing, plane the end grain straight and square, being careful to avoid splitting the far edge. Either lightly chamfer the edge first or else plane from alternate directions, each time stopping short of the far edge.

MARKING TAILS

Start by marking out the edges of the tails and the sockets between them, in which the pins will fit. If you want to make the inner pins fine, the openings of the sockets between tails can be as little as a single saw kerf wide.

The end pins must have sufficient thickness for strength so I suggest the edges of the outer tails are set at least ⅜in (10mm) from the sides. The gap between the end pins is then marked in two places to form three tails, or three places to form four tails etc. There are many different methods of laying out the positions of tails and it does not really matter which you use, as this is an issue of appearance and subjective opinion and will not affect the fit. For example, you can use a ruler and calculator to create equal divisions, slant a ruler

until the diagonal length makes division easy, or just position the tails by eye. After marking the socket centres, angled lines are scribed from them to mark the tail sides. For hardwood, it is common to slope the tail sides at an angle of 1:8 and a ready-made 'dovetail square' makes this easy, although a sliding bevel gauge would allow you to choose other angles. Scribe the edges of the sockets at right angles across the end grain.

The shoulder line marking the base of the socket between tails must be at a distance from the end equal to the corresponding wood thickness. Adjust a marking gauge to the thickness of the pin board (sycamore) and use this setting to score the shoulder line onto the tail board (brown oak).

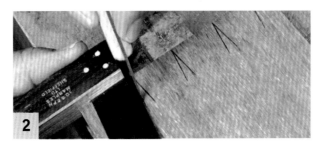

1 Mark out the positions of the sockets between tails.

2 Scribe the tails against an angled 'dovetail square'.

3 Scribe the edges of the sockets across the end grain.

CUTTING TAILS

Clamp the wood low in a vice so it cannot vibrate. The shoulder line should be just sufficiently clear of the bench to avoid clipping it. Use the finger and thumbnails of your free hand to guide the sawblade, ready for the first stroke.

For fine pins, use the same starting kerf twice, tilting the saw to produce the two sides to each socket. If you cut all the right-hand tail sides, then all the left-hand tail sides, your wrist can be locked to the appropriate angle. This also helps you concentrate with positioning the kerf just to the waste side of the line each time.

Clamp the wood sideways to be able to saw the end shoulders, with the kerf following the waste side of the knife line.

With all the tail sides sawn, remove the socket waste with a fretsaw or fine coping saw, then clean back to the shoulder line with a narrow bevel-edged chisel. Paring accurately can be tricky and it helps if you clamp the tails under a square-sided block of timber, aligned with the shoulder mark. Use this to guide the chisel, both to the correct position and the correct angle.

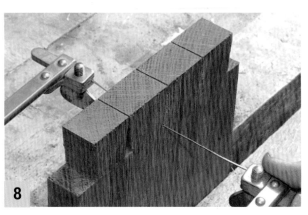

4 Use the finger and thumbnails to guide the sawblade, ready for the first stroke.

5 Clamp the oak low in the vice and with the saw tilted, follow the line on the right-hand side of each socket.

6 Using the same starting kerf, tilt the saw the other way to follow the line on the left side of each socket.

7 Clamp the wood sideways to saw the end shoulders, with the kerf following the waste side of the knife line.

8 Remove the socket waste with a frame saw, then clean back to the shoulder line with a fine chisel.

MARKING SOCKETS

Lay a plane on its side next to the vice and clamp the pin wood (sycamore) so its top is level with the plane. Now move the plane away from the vice and lay the tail wood (oak) on it to position the tails on the pin wood (sycamore) end grain. The tail shoulder line must lie directly on the vertical edge of the wood. The tails act as a template to allow marking out the pins, and accuracy is crucial at this stage. A fine marking knife is essential. The two pieces of wood must not be allowed to move during this operation, as any gap between the tail and the mark for the pin will convert directly into slack in the finished joint. The shoulder lines for the pins are marked just as they were for the tails, but this time, set the gauge to the thickness of the tail wood.

CUTTING SOCKETS

With the pins marked out, clamp the sycamore low in the vice. With the saw blade vertical, angle it horizontally to follow the direction of the pin marks and saw vertical kerfs on the waste side of each line. Again, it helps to concentrate on keeping the angle correct and staying on the waste side of the line, if you complete one side of every pin before you start on the other sides.

As with the tails, the socket bases need to be sawn away then cleaned with a chisel. Clamp a rectangular guide block against the shoulder line to keep the chisel vertical while paring to the line, this time using the widest chisel that will pass between the pins.

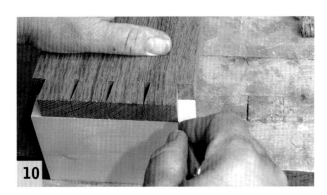

9 Lay a plane on its side next to the vice, and clamp the sycamore with its top level with the plane.

11 Clamp the sycamore low in the vice, and saw vertical kerfs on the waste side of each pin.

10 Move the plane away from the vice. Lay the oak on it to position the tails on the sycamore end grain, using them as a template to mark out the pins.

12 Clamp a rectangular guide block against the shoulder line to keep the chisel vertical while paring to the line.

FITTING THE JOINT

There is very little margin between a joint that is slack so it wobbles around and has unsightly gaps, and one that is too tight to fit together without risk of breaking. To help guide the joint together, chamfer the inside corners of each tail using a sharp chisel. Start the chamfer below the tail's end and finish it on the shoulder line so there will not be any visible gaps created by it. The first stage of fitting the pins into the sockets by hand allows the tightness to be felt.

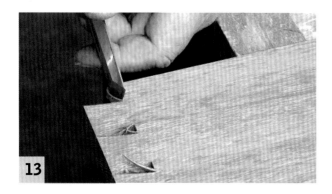

13 Chamfer the inside corners of each tail to lead the pins into the sockets.

14 The first stage of fitting by hand enables the tightness to be felt.

15 Check there are no gaps inside the joint.

Dovetails should be moderately tight, so do not force them before you glue up, otherwise separating them may cause damage. Just fit them partway so you can work them apart by hand. Glue is only needed to prevent dovetails from sliding loose or working apart – the strength and rigidity comes from the actual joint. With glue applied inside the sockets, the joint can be pressed together tightly with cramps, or knocked together with a mallet. Lay the joint on a flat reference surface and check for squareness while there is still time to make small adjustments. Dovetails do not need clamping while the glue sets. After the glue has set, run a fine block plane across each face of the joint to clean it up. Work the plane at an angle so it slices onto the wood edges. Never plane off the edges as this may cause splitting. Planing the joint can be a moment of revelation, enabling you to scrutinize the results. Chisels straying from vertical while paring shoulders can easily cause gaps, so check inside the joint as well. It can be a pleasant surprise to uncover the crisp edges of the joint from under a gluey mess, but even when the dovetails have not worked out as well as hoped, planing them improves the appearance.

SECRET MITRE DOVETAILS

Mark all the pin and tail ends of the table-top frame components ready for joining using a marker gauge as follows:

1 Mark a line across the inside of the joint, one timber's thickness distance from the end. This will form the shoulder line for the dovetails.

2 Mark a line one-quarter of the thickness from the end to form the transition between the top of the dovetails and the inner edge of the mitre.

3 Mark a line across the end grain at a quarter of the thickness in from the outer face.

With the saw positioned on line 2, cut a rebate across each end to the depth of line 3. Now make 45° knife lines on the edges for the mitre and use a dovetail saw to cut the sides of the mitres. Take the boards which will form the long sides of the frame and mark out the dovetail pins. Saw the pin sides and chop out the waste from the sockets between them with a narrow, razor-sharp chisel. Press the pins against the other half of the joint and use their sides as a

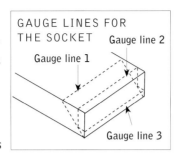

GAUGE LINES FOR THE SOCKET

Gauge line 1

Gauge line 2

Gauge line 3

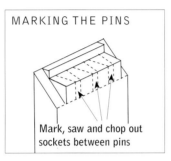

MARKING THE PINS

Mark, saw and chop out sockets between pins

template to knife mark the sides of the tails. Saw and chop the tails in the same way as the pins. Finally, with the board clamped edgewise in a vice at 45°, plane the mitre across the outside edge of each joint using a fine shoulder plane before trying the two halves of each joint together for a dry fit.

16 Mark the ends of components ready for the corners.

17 Saw a rebate across the end then saw the sides of the dovetail pins.

18 Chop out the sockets between pins with a fine chisel.

19 Use the sides of the dovetail pins as stencils to mark out the tails.

20 With tails sawn and chopped, plane away the mitre outside the joint.

21 Two sides of a secret mitred dovetail ready for fitting.

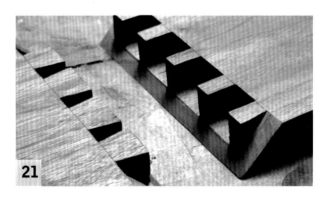

Making drawers

A drawer is a specialized type of open-topped box, which experiences frequent pushing and pulling from the front. This would make any box liable to deteriorate unless it was correctly designed and constructed for the purpose.

Good drawer fronts are usually attached with lapped dovetails, also known as half-blind dovetails because when they are assembled the tails are visible on one face only. These joints transmit the load from the sides into the front without weakening, as witnessed by the survival of many well-used antique drawers.

ABOVE The cabinet joints are through dovetails while the drawer joints are lapped dovetails.

Drawer backs in good-quality work are fixed with through dovetails, although being trapped between cabinet sides or rails to prevent sideways movement and not being pushed or pulled by the user means they experience much less strain than the fronts.

TECHNICAL TIP

Drawer sides should be made with stable timber, such as well-dried quarter-sawn oak. This avoids cupping or bowing, which could jam the drawer. Sides are preferably made thinner than the front to keep down weight and friction.

JARGON BUSTING

lapped dovetails – recessed dovetail used for drawer fronts, also known as 'half-blind'.

CARCASSES FOR DRAWERS

It is normal to make a furniture carcass first before planing the front, back and side parts of a drawer to fit the aperture. Drawer dovetails are cut by hand for fine cabinet work, alternatively with a router to produce equally sturdy, but arguably less attractive-looking joints. The drawer is then assembled before fine-tuning it to fit the carcass.

When closed, the drawer front sits between drawer rails above and below, or in some cases the cabinet base or top. A conventional drawer rides between upper and lower side rails known as kickers and runners respectively. Guides prevent sideways movement, or sometimes the sides of the cabinet do this job. Chests of drawers may include dust-boards as horizontal dividing panels.

1 Fit the drawer front, side and backs to the carcass before making up drawers.

2 Drawer dovetails cut with a router jig – lapped at the front, through at the rear.

3

4

3 Glued-up drawers are planed to a fine fit before waxing.

4 Runners are screwed or glued at the front, screwed in slotted holes at the rear.

Guides and rails may be mortice and tenoned into front and back drawer rails or alternatively screwed in place. In either method there can be a conflict in grain direction with carcass parts, in which case the back rail joints are left unglued or the screw-holes slotted. This traditional method of construction allows drawer sides to be made thin and very light in weight, which also reduces the depth of the dovetail joints.

Alternatively, a single rail may run in a slot that is routed along each drawer side. This method provides all six sliding guide surfaces with one pair of rails. While it requires the sides to be thicker, this method simplifies construction and works well with some designs.

HAND-CUT LAPPED DOVETAILS

Cutting the lapped tails on drawer sides is similar to cutting basic through dovetails, but the lapped sockets on the drawer front are quite different. Each tail of the lapped dovetail joint is tucked into a four-sided socket so only the sides of the tail show, and even that is only when the drawer is pulled open.

All precision joints, especially dovetails, need the timber to be carefully faced and edged with square ends before starting. Additionally, before making a drawer, the front, sides and back must be carefully planed to fit the appropriate place in the carcass aperture. The fit should be tight at this stage to

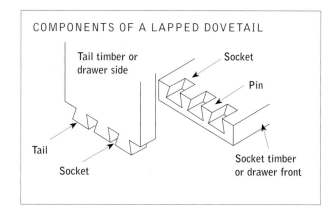

COMPONENTS OF A LAPPED DOVETAIL

Tail timber or drawer side

Socket

Pin

Tail

Socket

Socket timber or drawer front

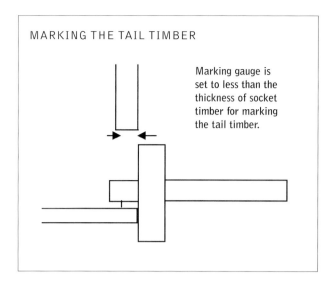

MARKING THE TAIL TIMBER

Marking gauge is set to less than the thickness of socket timber for marking the tail timber.

allow further trimming after assembly. The parts must be labelled after fitting so they will be assembled in the correct orientation.

SHOULDER LINES

The position of the shoulder is the most critical line for marking out lapped dovetails. Corresponding lines must be marked at the same depth on both pieces so the depth of the tails will match the depth of their sockets. For the lapped dovetails, set your marking gauge to less than the thickness of the socket timber by typically ¼in (6mm). Mark the shoulders of the pins and the tails with lines across each side of the tail timber and without changing the gauge setting, mark a corresponding line across the end of the socket timber.

CUTTING LAPPED DOVETAILS

Clamp the tail wood low in a vice so it cannot vibrate, and tilt it slightly so that the tail mark runs vertically. This allows you to hold the saw straight while cutting the sloping sides. If, for example, you cut all the left tail sides first then cut all the right tail sides, you only need to re-clamp the wood once. This also helps you concentrate on positioning the saw just to the waste side of the line each time.

With all the tail sides sawn, use a coping saw, or a fretsaw for fine dovetails, to remove the socket waste, keeping the saw cut about ⅟₁₆in (2mm) above the shoulder line. Take a sharp, narrow chisel and pare the tail sockets back to the shoulder line.

Paring accurately can be tricky at first and it helps if you clamp the tails under a square-sided block of timber, aligned with the shoulder mark. You can use this to guide the chisel both to the correct position and to the correct angle.

MARKING LAPPED DOVETAIL SOCKETS

Once you have marked the shoulder line for the sockets, lay a plane on its side next to the vice and clamp the socket wood vertically so its end is level with the upper side of the plane. Move the plane away from the vice to act as an end support and lay the tails with the shoulders just on top of the vertical edge of the clamped timber. Line up the ends of the tails with the shoulder line that will form the base of the sockets. Use a fine knife or scalpel to mark carefully around each side of each tail in the end grain.

5

5 Use a scalpel to mark carefully around each side and the end of each tail.

SAWING LAPPED DOVETAIL SOCKETS

With the sockets marked, clamp the wood edgewise in the vice and tilt it away so you can see both the face and end grain. Saw down the inside edge of each knife line on both face and end at once. Repeat this for each side of each socket.

Remove the timber from the vice and clamp it firmly down onto the bench top. Using a razor-sharp chisel that is narrower than the socket, chop lightly just inside the shoulder line about $\frac{1}{16}$in (2mm) deep to begin to form the base of the socket then, with the chisel edge in the end grain, pare away a thin shaving right up to the chopped shoulder line. Chop again at the base of the socket and alternate between chopping the shoulder line and paring along the end grain, so that you progressively deepen the socket.

6

7

8

The final shavings are pared back to the shoulder lines and the corners cleaned out to leave flat-based sockets with angled sides corresponding to the tails. Test fit the joints as you complete them. They should be tight so do not force them all the way home, otherwise separating them to apply glue may cause damage. Only fit them part way so you can work them apart by hand.

TRIAL-FITTING DRAWERS

Whether the joints are hand cut or router made, the drawer will need careful fitting to the carcass aperture. If you use a comb template router jig that only produces half-blind dovetails, you will need to make the back thicker to receive them.

Guide rails are either dry mortice and tenoned or screwed inside the carcass to carry the drawers. The screw-holes at the front are round but at the middle and back they are elongated and the screw-fitted halfway along. This allows seasonal movement of the carcass side panels without the risk of self-destructive splitting.

The glued up drawers are planed to a fine fit before waxing their sides and the carcass lining with beeswax furniture paste to reduce friction.

DRAWER BASES

The base of a drawer is traditionally made with a thin panel of softwood, in which case side-to-side grain orientation and slotted fitting with room for expansion at the back are important features. Cedar of Lebanon is preferred because of its permanent fresh smell and repellence to insects. Base panels can be made from stable man-made boards such as plywood or cedar-veneered MDF for easier construction. Slots for the base may be cut directly in the drawer sides if they are thick enough, otherwise thin batons of hardwood known as drawer slips are glued on the sides to prevent weakening the lower edges.

6 Saw down the inside edge of each knife line on both face and end at once.

7 Chop lightly just inside the shoulder line.

8 Pare a thin shaving to the chopped shoulder line.

9 The socket corners are cleaned out with a bevel-edged chisel.

10 Fit the lapped dovetails partway so you can work them apart by hand.

Dust extraction

After machining or sanding wood, you often see dust in rays of sunlight. Fine particles hang in the air for hours and can be seriously hazardous to health. A good dust extraction system will solve this problem.

Every workshop has a kind of different layout and equipment with different extraction requirements so it is important to grasp the principles of dust control before installing a system. There are two main types of extractor.

DUST AND CHIPPING EXTRACTORS

These extractors use a large centrifugal impeller to move a large quantity of air. Flow rates typically range from 500 to 5000 cubic metres per hour. Air, wood dust and chippings all pass through the impeller which must be sturdy to survive hits from offcuts. The mixture is blown into a pair of bags where the air slows down and larger chippings drop into the lower collecting sack while dust is blown through the filter on top. Dust and chipping

ABOVE Low flow causes woodchips to accumulate in the corrugations of a duct.

1

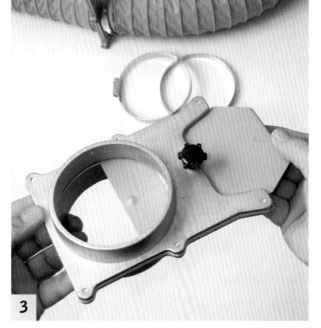

extractors can shift large volumes, provided there is not too much restriction but they do not cope well with small pipes or fine filters. The cloth bags often supplied as standard, let dust through so there is an option of fitting a fine filter bag or a filter cartridge. A one-micron bag can reduce the airflow by 35% and needs regular cleaning, but produces a healthier atmosphere.

FINE DUST EXTRACTORS

These are high-pressure low volume extractors that work like a heavily constructed domestic vacuum cleaner. Flow rates range from 200 to 400 cubic metres per hour. They use a small multi-stage turbine turned by a high-speed brushed motor to suck air through a collection bag or filter. Only filtered air passes through the turbine making this type of extractor suitable for collecting fine dust from sanders but they shift a smaller volume. The machine may clog up with large chippings and the bag may quickly fill. Fine dust extractors can be relatively noisy and heat up in use while many are not continuously rated.

PIPE LOSSES

Larger workshops have plumbed-in systems with long ducts, 'T' and 'Y' connectors and blast gates to direct the flow. If it is necessary to place the

1 The dust and chipping extractor has a large centrifugal steel impeller.

2 Dust from sanders and small machines can be collected with a fine dust extractor or industrially rated vacuum cleaner.

3 Blast gates allow you to shut off unused flow paths.

extractor some distance from the machine, rigid smooth-bore pipes impose less of a restriction. Alternatively, if an extractor is on wheels and the floor is flat it is quite practical to move it between machines, connecting to each with a push-fit adaptor. This keeps duct lengths short and avoids complicated installations. The recommended minimum air speed for collecting woodchips and dust from machines is 10 metres per second. Wood dust starts to move in a smooth straight pipe when the air speed is 3 metres per second, but in corrugated pipes it takes 5 metres per second to start and clears the pipe at 7 metres per second. Once chippings start to accumulate in a duct they restrict the flow further, quickly leading to blockage.

See page 188 for a table showing a comparison of flow rates in different units and speeds in different tube sizes.

Planers and thicknessers

The process of choosing and using planers and thicknessers can be daunting for the beginner cabinetmaker, so here is some sound advice to help you be able to decide what to buy and how to use it well.

Planers and thicknessers take the donkeywork out of stock preparation, saving your energy for the more creative tasks. You can buy two separate pieces of kit – a surface planer (or jointer) and a thicknesser but often the planer thicknesser comes as a dual-function (over and under) machine. This makes sense because both parts do essentially the same job of removing a layer of shavings, leaving a flat surface. The difference is in the way the wood is supported – when you are surface planing, the wood is passed over the cutter block between the infeed and outfeed tables, flattening the underside. When thicknessing, the wood is rested on the thicknessing table and passed under the cutter block flattening the top surface. The essential features of the planer thicknesser were standardized many years

ABOVE A planer/thicknesser blade is clamped on a grinder and height adjusted to keep the same grinding angle.

ago but there are choices in width, features and quality of construction. Cast iron is the preferred material for machine tables because its weight and stiffness resist vibration.

JARGON BUSTING

rowed – striped wood with naturally alternating grain direction.
whetstone – grindstone or sharpening stone.

The main parts of a planer/ thicknesser

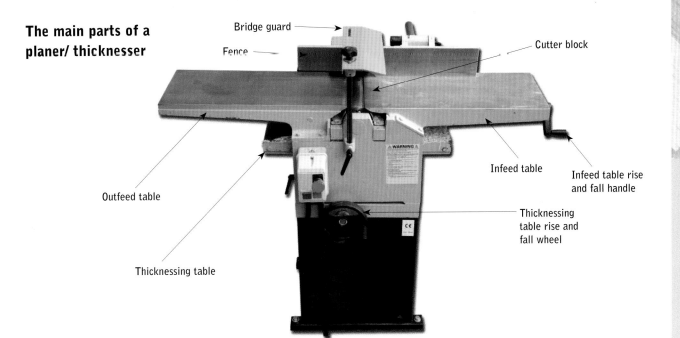

Bridge guard

Fence

Cutter block

Outfeed table

Infeed table

Infeed table rise and fall handle

Thicknessing table rise and fall wheel

Thicknessing table

FACE AND EDGE

The processes of machine facing and edging timber are directly equivalent to the techniques previously learned with a hand plane – namely create a flat surface then produce an opposite parallel face and an edge at right angles to it.

Start by laying the rough face of the wood down on a planer table and passing it over the cutter block for the underside to be flattened. This new face will be the reference plane for all the other surfaces and joints, so its quality sets the standard. Next, lay this flattened face down on the thicknesser table and pass it back under the cutter block to create a parallel flat surface on the upper face. Rather than slicing long continuous shavings as the hand plane does, machines remove a series of scoops from the surface so closely spaced they almost blend together as a flat surface.

EDGE PLANING

The planer has a vertical fence running above the infeed and outfeed tables. The flat face of the timber will be used as a reference surface by pressing it sideways against the fence while passing the lower edge along the planer table. You can check the angle of the fence with an engineering square and adjust it

if necessary. The fence usually has a variable angle and a preset end-stop for 90° position. After surface planing, the board is turned edge-down onto the planer table and its face pressed against a side fence to produce a straight perpendicular lower edge. If the wood is thick enough, this edge can be stood on the thicknesser table and passed through the thicknesser to create the opposite parallel edge. For thin wood, the second edge must be produced against the planer fence.

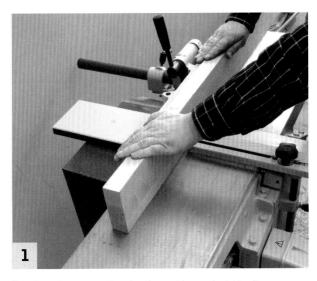

1 Edge plane pressing the face side against the fence.

SAFETY PRECAUTIONS

While thicknessers automatically feed wood past the cutter, planers are described as 'hand-fed' machines. There are some serious safety issues to learn before using any woodworking machine and 'hand-fed' machines in particular. The hands-on aspects of safe machine work are best learnt at a college, while the specific safety requirements for any machine should be in its manual. The most important points are to fit the guards correctly, use push sticks and blocks where appropriate, and watch out for trailing clothes, jewellery or hair. Fingers not in use should be tucked away or over the fence so that they cannot trail. Before carrying out any adjustment or maintenance, the electrical supply must first be isolated.

PREPARING TO SURFACE PLANE

The wood is passed along the infeed table over the cutter block, which removes the rough lower surface, leaving a flat face to slide along the outfeed table. The depth of cut on the planer is increased by lowering the infeed table. Typically about ⅛in (3mm) can be removed on the initial cut, reducing to ¹⁄₃₂in (1mm) or less for fine surfacing. You will need to decide first which face of the wood to pass over the planer. By sighting along the edge of a board you can see if there is any bowing or cupping and place the hollow side down so that the wood does not rock on the table. Arrange the wood so that the grain slopes up towards the cutter block. This is not always possible, particularly if the grain direction changes.

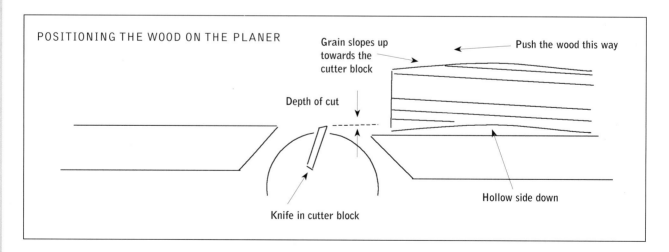

POSITIONING THE WOOD ON THE PLANER

Grain slopes up towards the cutter block

Push the wood this way

Depth of cut

Knife in cutter block

Hollow side down

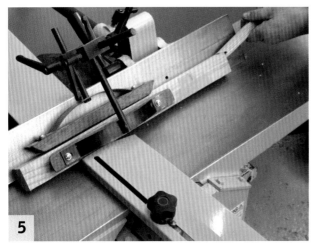

2 Start planing with both hands over the infeed table.

3 Move the left hand forward over the outfeed table.

4 The push block is used when planing short pieces of timber.

5 Small pieces of timber are fed though Shaw guards, using a push stick.

While the planer's finish is inherently less smooth than good hand-plane work, the short, curved strokes made by the knives in the cutter block make it more forgiving of grain direction, and any tear marks around awkward grain tend to be shorter.

FEEDING A PLANER

To use the planer, stand alongside the infeed table with feet 12in (300mm) apart. The bridge guard must cover the cutter block at all times. It is designed to be raised on a pillar or swinging arm to allow the wood to pass between guard and cutter. The gap between wood and guard should be set as small as possible. Start feeding the planer with both hands pressing the timber onto the infeed table. Once 6in (150mm) or so of wood has emerged from beneath the bridge guard, move the left hand forward to press it onto the outfeed table. Continue to feed with one hand each side of the guard until the infeed end is short, and then finish with both hands pressing on the outfeed table.

Try to avoid planing pieces shorter than 12in (300mm) as there is insufficient length to apply hand pressure each side of the guard. If you do need to plane a short piece, use a push block to apply the pressure. Make the push block from a length of hardwood with a set of plane handles attached. The underside of the push block has sandpaper glued on and a strip of hardwood at the back end, which will enable you to guide the timber beneath.

The fence, which is normally fixed at right angles to the tables, can be tilted to create a chamfered edge on the timber. However, this does make the wood likely to slide off the fence which can be risky, particularly with small-section timber. The safe way to carry out this task is using Shaw guards. These are pairs of sprung wooden pressure pads forming a tunnel around the fence and cutter. The timber is fed under the Shaw guards using a push stick, simply made from an offcut with a V-notch sawn in the end.

THICKNESSING

Beneath the planer tables, the thicknessing table can be raised and lowered in height to adjust the thickness of wood produced. The height is adjusted to remove $\frac{5}{64}$–$\frac{1}{8}$in (2–3mm) at a single pass. If you only need to remove the unevenness left by timber conversion, a single pass is enough, otherwise the wood may be reduced in stages to the thickness required for a project. Arrange the grain direction to fall towards the cutter block and as with surface planing, it may be necessary to compromise on awkward or rowed wood by making light cuts in alternate directions.

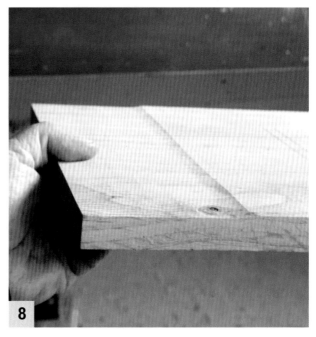

6 Beneath the planer tables, the thicknessing table can be raised and lowered in height.

7 From left to right: timber passes beneath anti-kickback fingers, is grabbed by the serrated infeed roller, passed under the cutter block and then beneath the smooth outfeed roller.

8 End snipe is a common problem when thicknessing.

KNIVES

Cutter blocks are fitted with two to four knives, three being the most common number on medium-sized machines. Keeping a spare set of knives means you will not be delayed for long in the middle of a project or tempted to struggle on with dull edges.

High-speed steel knives hold a good edge and are relatively easy to sharpen (see box on page 76). If you keep them razor sharp and nick-free, the finish will be excellent, requiring minimal hand planing or sanding afterwards. Tungsten carbide knives hold an edge for longer but initially they are not as sharp and so they produce a relatively poor finish. Some TCT knives can be resharpened but they take longer than steel. The procedure for removing and replacing blades takes a bit of learning, after which it can be done quite quickly. Disposable blades are available for some machines, but the quality is not always up to the standard for fine work. Tersa cutter blocks fitted on some machines use a self-clamping arrangement where the knife-retaining bar is held in place by centrifugal force, making changing quick and easy.

9 The planer knife accessory on a workshop grinder.

10 Release the knives from the cutter block for sharpening or replacement.

11 Steel knives will lift out with a magnet.

SHARPENING PLANER KNIVES

Resharpenable knives must be removed from the machine for sharpening if the edges are blunt, have been honed a few times or have been chipped by use on mineral contaminated wood.

Each knife is clamped beneath a cutter block, held by a set of retaining screws which may be loosened with an Allen key or spanner. A magnet is useful for lifting the knives. Keep the chip-breakers and knives in sequence by marking them if necessary. Some of the better models of workshop grinder have an optional attachment for sharpening planer knives. This holds the knife at a fixed height and angle as you slide it back and forth across the grinding wheel, producing a new sharp, straight edge. There may be a wire edge left on the knife which you can strop on a leather belt or hone away on wet and dry paper.

I made a simple jig from plywood to hold knives at a constant angle while I rub them against wet and dry paper laid on a sheet of float glass. This gives a superb razor-sharp edge after grinding on the wheel. If you don't have a suitable wheel, with a little extra time and patience, a jig like this can be used for sharpening blades by working through grades of wet and dry paper.

POSITIONING OF PLANER KNIVES

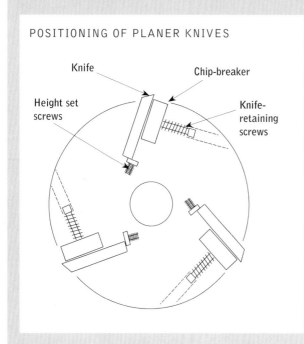

Knife

Chip-breaker

Height set screws

Knife-retaining screws

12

13

12 A workshop-made jig clamps the knife at a fixed angle.

13 Honing against fine wet and dry paper on thick glass gives a razor-sharp edge.

HONING

If a resharpenable knife edge isn't too dull or damaged, it can be honed on the machine, saving a good deal of time. This is best done with a thick, flat, diamond whetstone laid on the infeed table. Lower the infeed table and rotate the cutter block so the bevel angle of a knife passes just above it. Wedge the cutter block in place with an offcut and lay a piece of paper on the infeed table to protect it. The knife edge is then lightly honed by repeatedly pulling the stone over the bevel edge into the infeed table. Lift the stone and move further along the knife with each stroke. Do not push the stone into the edge as it will dig in or scrape off the surface.

The resulting secondary bevel will be at a coarser angle and as a result of this, it will be stronger and less susceptible to damage than the original edge. However, this will also increase friction causing the knife edge to heat more, and it may burnish the wood. The solution is to keep the secondary bevel small by only honing on the machine lightly and occasionally.

REPLACING KNIVES

After sharpening or replacement, the knives are clamped beneath the chip-breaker bar which is held in the cutter block by retaining bolts. These may be loosely clamped while the knives are adjusted. Resharpenable knives need to be adjusted in height by a pair of set screws beneath the ends of each one. The tip of the knife should just rise above the outfeed table height at the very top of its stroke. To check this, lay a straight edge on the outfeed table and turn the cutter block by hand. Each knife should lift the straight edge almost invisibly and drag it along a distance of $\frac{3}{16}$in (5mm). Check this at each end of the knife to ensure it is level.

Tighten the retaining screws starting at the middle and working towards each end. The knives can accidentally move while being tightened, so check again with a straight edge afterwards. With everything checked and the guard replaced, you can restore the power supply.

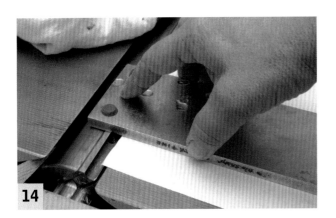

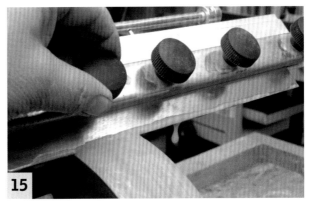

14 With the machine isolated and cutter block wedged, the knives can be lightly honed in situ.

15 Sliding the cutter from side to side, the fixed geometry of the grinder gives a straight edge to the knife.

16 Rock the knife backwards and forwards in its cutter block while adjusting the set screw beneath. A ruler on edge rides forward a few millimetres as the knife passes beneath.

Circular sawbench

Furniture-makers' timber was always sawn by hand until Victorian times when circular saw blade mills became widely used. These days we are spoilt for choice with a range of sturdy and reliable floor-standing machinery.

Sawbenches come in many shapes and sizes and with various names. They comprise of a flat, sturdy table with a circular sawblade protruding up through a slot. Machines with a large sliding table or carriage to the side of the blade, are described as panel saws or sometimes dimension saws. If the workshop has enough space and a suitable budget, these big machines are a boon to accurate furniture making, but not if they get in the way of other tasks. Small table saws are designed for standing on the bench or, when legs are fitted, they are sold as contractors' saws or site saws. While handy for construction work, these do not have enough weight and rigidity for use in furniture-making. Fortunately, in between, there is a whole range of sturdy floor-standing machines that may be referred

ABOVE With the blade set low, a large number of teeth are cutting at any time.

to as cabinet saws. We will look at using these in a cabinetmaker's workshop where boards need to be rip-sawn along the grain into suitable widths, and crosscut into accurate lengths ready for planing, shaping and jointing.

JARGON BUSTING

kickback – wood thrown by a machine when it accidentally catches the blade.
arbor – the spindle carrying a cutter or blade.

Main parts of the sawbench

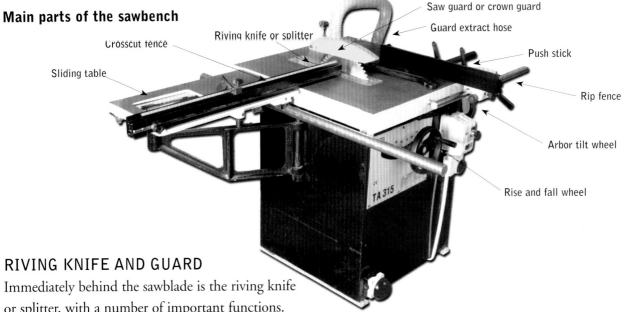

Saw guard or crown guard
Guard extract hose
Crosscut fence
Riving knife or splitter
Sliding table
Push stick
Rip fence
Arbor tilt wheel
TA 315
Rise and fall wheel

RIVING KNIFE AND GUARD

Immediately behind the sawblade is the riving knife or splitter, with a number of important functions. The main purpose of this fin-shaped steel plate, which rises and falls as you adjust the blade height, is to prevent tension trapped in the freshly sawn wood from closing up on the back edge of the blade. While the leading edge of the sawblade presses wood down against the table, the up-cutting teeth at the back edge try to lift it, and then the top of the blade tries to push it towards the front of the table.

The riving knife also prevents assistants from accidental contact with the rear of the blade while handling wood on the outfeed side of the table. The riving knife is usually designed to support the blade guard or crown guard. This device helps prevent accidents from timber or hands contacting the blade top, and it collects dust thrown out by the vortex wind around the blade, feeding this into the extractor.

1 Using a sliding table to crosscut oak board.

2 The riving knife, which is bolted to the arbor carriage, rises and falls with the blade and the crown guard.

3 The crown guard is lowered as close to the wood as it is practical.

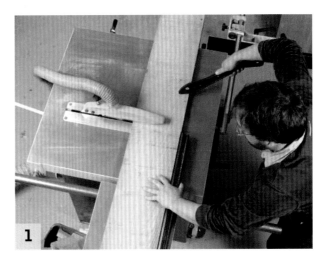

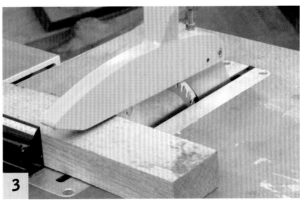

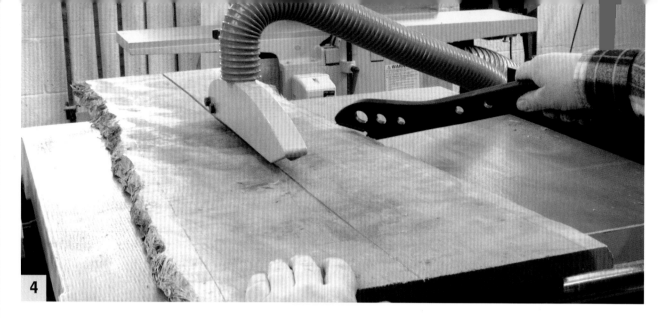

4 The first rip-cut is made down the pith line.

FIRST CUT

If you start with waney-edged timber that still has the bark on, or with square-edged boards that have been distorted at the edge by the drying process, there will be no reference edge to guide against a fence. This means you need to mark out the cutting line and follow it by eye with both fences out of the way, taking care not to make movements that could jam the blade.

FENCES

Sawbenches are equipped with two fences to guide the movement of the wood: one running parallel to the blade for use with ripsaw cuts, and a sliding

SAFETY PRECAUTIONS

Modern sawbenches are safe when they are used correctly – the hands-on aspects of safe machine work are best learnt at college while the specific safety requirements for any machine are in the manual. The most important points are to fit the guards correctly, use push sticks within 12in (300mm) of the blade, keep out of line with the blade, and prevent situations where the wood can jam.

TECHNICAL TIP

A circular sawblade edge typically travels at 100 miles per hour (50 metres per second) with enough momentum behind it to launch offcuts of timber at the same speed! With kickbacks like this in mind, experienced users stand to one side of the blade, out of the path of missiles.

fence at right angles to the blade for crosscuts. The rip fence can be positioned at any position from the blade up to the maximum rip width. There is a scale to indicate the nominal width of the sawn material and, when getting to know a machine, it is worth checking just how accurate this is, then you will know if you can depend on it or if it needs adjusting.

Wood can be trapped between the rip fence and the blade with disastrous results if the fence is adjusted too far back, particularly if it contacts the wood when crosscutting. The solution is to set the back edge of the rip fence in line with the blade centre, or move it completely out of the way when crosscutting.

Depending on the design and capacity of the machine, the crosscut fence can vary from a large swinging arm or sliding table, to a small guide running in a groove on the table. The user holds

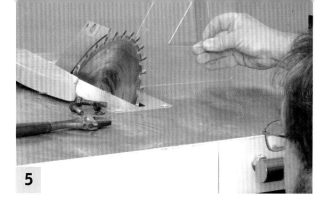

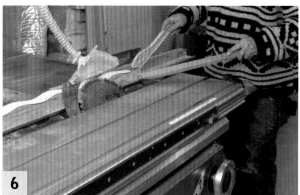

the timber tightly against the crosscut fence and slides the fence forward while feeding it into the blade. If the offcut end is long, use the push stick to move it and prevent splintering at the end of the cut.

ANGLED CUTS

The crosscut fence can usually be angled or have an angle attachment fitted to enable horizontally mitred ends to be produced. The blade is normally perpendicular to the table but on most sawbenches, it can be tilted at an angle of up to 45°, allowing you to rip bevelled edges or crosscut vertically mitred ends. To permit this, the manufacturers fix both the motor and the arbor – the shaft or spindle carrying the blade – beneath the table on a hinged swinging frame. The angle of this frame is adjusted with a handle and there is usually a calibrated dial to show how many degrees the sawblade is set to.

However, small errors in angled cuts can accumulate when you join a number of them to make a box for example, so for accurate work, it is preferable to use the scale on the saw for coarse adjustment only, then fine-tune it with a setsquare. The rip fence will obstruct the angled sawblade if it is placed too close. On most machines this can be avoided by laying the fence on its side to lower it.

BLADES

Just as with handsaws, there are optimum designs of blades for ripping and crosscutting hardwoods as well as others for manufactured boards. The ripping blade has widely spaced teeth with large gullets between, allowing quantities of dust to be removed and permitting a high feed rate. Crosscut blades have closely pitched teeth to provide fine finish and reduce splintering.

In practice, the small workshop often uses a single machine to alternate between ripping and crosscut operations, so a compromise is called for, and many good general-purpose blades are available. Some machines have a scoring blade in

5 A tilting arbor enables the saw to cut accurate mitres.

6 Using push sticks to make an angled ripsaw cut.

7 Beneath the table, a sealed induction motor drives the arbor (top left) through belts and pulleys.

line with the main blade and just ahead of it. The small-diameter blade runs in the opposite direction from the main blade, cutting the lower surface to eliminate the risk of splintering. This feature is particularly useful on man-made laminate boards.

Good-quality blades are worth the extra money. Each tooth takes away a very small amount of material at a single pass, so if any tooth is longer

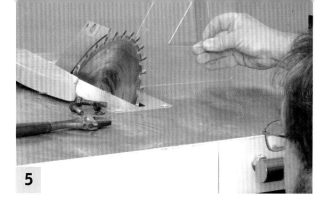

than its neighbours, then it will do all the work. Similarly, any misalignment due to blade distortion, will cause an uneven finish and uneven wear on the blade, reducing its life dramatically. Dull-edged blades work slowly, producing a poor finish and increase the force required, increasing the risk of accidents. Blades can be sent away to be resharpened, but the job requires precision equipment.

BLADE TIPS

Most modern blades have tungsten carbide tips brazed onto the shaped edge of a precision steel disk. Early designs of tungsten carbide tipped blades, while longer lasting, did not have the sharpness of alloy steel so they tended to be reserved for man-made boards. However, they have improved to the extent that most makers now only use TCT blades.

Because the tips are wider than the steel part of the blade, they produce a wider kerf, so there is no need for the teeth to be 'set' or angled to prevent jamming. A popular design has alternate bevelled tips so that every other tip severs fibres on each side of the kerf, producing a very clean crosscut. Triple chip blades are designed to alternate between teeth that cut the edges of the kerf and teeth that remove material from the middle, again giving a fast, clean cut. Other kinds of blade tips such as polycrystalline diamond (PCD), are available for cutting very hard abrasive materials.

BLADE CHANGING

Removing the blade may require a table insert to be unscrewed first to give access to the arbor. The insert is usually made from aluminium or plastic, sometimes cabinetmakers will fit a wooden infill at the edge in order to try and prevent any slivers becoming trapped.

The blade is clamped between a flange fixed to the arbor and a loose flange trapped beneath the arbor nut. This nut is usually left-hand threaded

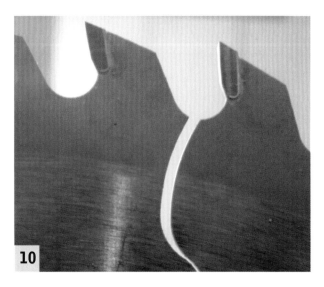

to prevent it working loose with the starting torque. The arbor must be locked to prevent it moving while the nut is loosened or tightened up.

TABLE ADJUSTMENTS

Movements of sliding crosscut tables must run precisely parallel to the blade. The rip fence must also lie parallel to the blade. Both these can be checked as part of the routine maintenance by

11

12

13

8 Coarse-toothed blades (left), designed for ripping, cut quickly but with a rough finish.

9 With the blade set high, a small number of teeth are cutting at any time.

10 An expansion gap is shaped to minimize distortion of the warm blade and reduce noise.

11 The arbor is locked in position for blade changing.

12 The left-handed nut tightens anticlockwise.

13 Sawdust drops into a hopper below and is funnelled into the extractor duct.

measuring the distance from the table to the teeth at the front and back of the blade, and both can be adjusted if necessary by moving the supports to make them true. Movements of a crosscut table must run level with the main table, and again this can be adjusted if necessary.

The blade must normally run vertical to the table surface, which you are able to check with an engineering square accurate to BS939. If the saw has a tilting arbor, the end stop for the tilt mechanism may need adjusting to bring it true. The riving knife must be rigidly mounted in line with the blade. Any misalignment must be corrected or if the knife is seriously bent, it must be replaced.

EXTRACTION

The table saw needs to be connected to a dust extractor (see page 68 for more details about dust extractors), which is turned on before sawing and runs on for a short time after sawing. The saw supplier will specify the capacity of extractor required. However, bear in mind that saws produce fine dust, requiring a fine filter to collect it, and this will reduce the dust extractor's efficiency.

Sawdust collects in the gullets between teeth on the circular sawblade and most of it is forced down under the table, where it is thrown out by centrifugal forces. A hopper-shaped chute beneath the table collects the dust and feeds it into the extract outlet. Ideally for dust collection, the air speed should be at least 10 metres per second. While even a small extractor can easily achieve this in a duct, the wide-open space of the hopper reduces the air speed here to much less. To make matters worse, slivers of offcuts that escape down the edge of the sawblade may jam in the extract duct and block the flow. The upshot of this is that dust will accumulate beneath the table and you need to give it a regular cleaning.

Bandsaws

Bandsaws are practically indispensable in most workshops. They are often the first machine a furniture-maker buys. They can rip-cut, crosscut, fair curves, slice veneers, cut joints and they occupy very little floorspace.

The bandsaw consists of a pair of vertically aligned wheels supported in an enclosed frame. The lower wheel is driven by an induction motor, usually through a V-belt and pulleys. The wheels are fitted with hard flat rubber tyres. The steel blade or 'band' runs between them as an endless loop. As the wheels turn, the vertical section of blade is drawn down through a slot in the table. The table is horizontal and can be tilted. It is usually made from cast iron to resist vibration. Fixed below the table are three guides, one behind the blade and one to each side of it, keeping the blade running true. Above the table is a similar set of guides mounted on an adjustable guide post. This allows the upper guides to be raised and lowered to accommodate different thicknesses of wood on the table.

ABOVE Ripping curved chair parts on the bandsaw.

Although simple and reliable, the bandsaw does require periodic maintenance and adjustment to give good service and be useful for precision work. Bandsaw blades need changing when the teeth are dull, the blade has been damaged or you are using the machine for a different type of work The guides, wheels and table will also need periodically adjusting.

JARGON BUSTING

gullets – the gaps between saw teeth.
feed rate – speed of wood fed into blades on a machine.

The main parts of a bandsaw

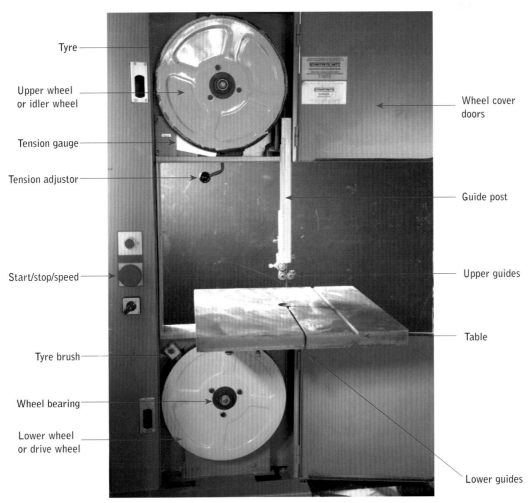

Tyre

Upper wheel
or idler wheel

Tension gauge

Tension adjustor

Start/stop/speed

Tyre brush

Wheel bearing

Lower wheel
or drive wheel

Wheel cover
doors

Guide post

Upper guides

Table

Lower guides

1 Bandsaws are practically indispensable in most
workshops and large ones are ideal for roughing out
components.

SAFETY PRECAUTIONS

Bandsaws have a reputation for being docile
machines, far less scary than a spindle moulder
for example, or a sawbench. However, even
bandsaws have their bad moments. One thing
to guard against is leaving a length of blade
exposed after making a deep cut. Another is
to avoid cutting unsupported material that is
not laid flat on the table – it can jam on the
blade and snatch violently. With careful use and
a little maintenance and adjustment, bandsaws
can give decades of service – in fact some
vintage models built early in the last century are
still in regular use by some established
furniture-makers.

BANDSAW BLADES

The bandsaw blade's back is strong and flexible to be able to withstand the continuous bending and straightening as it runs around the wheels. Blade material is manufactured as a continuous

2

3

2 Welded joint in the blade is ground flat by the supplier.

3 Unfolding a new bandsaw blade.

strip, normally cut to length and joined into a loop by the supplier. There is a welded joint forming the ends of the blade into a loop. This weld has considerable influence on the quality of the finished blade. If it is uneven, the front and back edges of the blade will be different lengths, making it unstable and tracking poorly on the wheels.

After welding the blade ends, the supplier will often grind the weld but may still leave a thick spot that can catch in the guides if they are closely adjusted. You might need to file this down, but do so cautiously. While the welded joint should be at least as strong as the rest of the blade because the metal is thicker there, the weld may not be fully penetrated in the gap and grinding it further can leave weak voids. During manufacture the blade is heat-treated on the front edge to harden the teeth and this can also affect the shape and tracking.

BANDSAW TEETH

Bandsaw blade teeth must be sharp and hard so they do not wear quickly. The very tip of the tooth can become extremely hot while cutting abrasive woods or manufactured sheet material. This softens the cutting edges, increasing susceptibility to wear and leading to distortion of the blade.

The pitch or spacing between teeth determines the feed rate at which the blade can cut, as well as the smoothness of the sawn surface. If there are too few teeth in the material they cause vibration and lead to a rough-sawn surface. As the number of

TECHNICAL TIP

Students sometimes avoid changing bandsaw blades, not just because of the cost, but also because they find the job a bit scary. Once you have folded and unfolded the blade a few times, it becomes easy to see how to avoid being grazed by it. If in any doubt, wear gardening gloves for the first few times.

4

4 Deep cutting collects large quantities of dust in the tooth gullets.

BANDSAW BLADE DRIFT

Small errors in the angles to which the teeth are set, mean that all blades have a bias or drift to one side or the other. For shallow kerfs, this may not be noticed but in the middle of a deep cut, it will cause the blade to twist, resulting in a cut that bellies out to one side.

To avoid this, estimate the blade's drift by finding the line it prefers to follow with a freehand cut. Use synthetic board such as MDF, because it has no grain to push the blade off course. Mark a line down the middle and follow it by eye, fine-tuning the angle of the board until you are confident it is cutting along the line. Now clamp the board to the table and slide the fence up against it with the fence's rail loosened, so that you can adjust the angle at which the fence crosses the table. Techniques for this vary quite a bit between makes. The fence should now be parallel to the blade's natural angle of cut.

teeth on a blade increases, the size of the gullets between the teeth reduces. The gullets are the areas between teeth that carry away sawdust, and the smaller these are the slower the blade can cut. If they are too small they choke with dust, and the blade overheats causing distortion and a poor cut.

The teeth are set (or bent) to right and left in an alternating sequence like on a handsaw. This creates a wider kerf and prevents the steel back from binding. It also allows the course of the blade to be varied slightly while cutting curves. Coarse blades with two or three teeth per inch (12–8mm tooth pitch) are best for re-sawing while less than

ten teeth per inch or more (3mm pitch) is most suitable for thin materials. Standard and skip-tooth blades have no rake angle, or to put it in other words the leading edge of the tooth is at right angles to the band. This gives them a slower cutting action compared to hook-tooth blades which have a positive rake angle making them able to cut more aggressively. Hook-tooth blades require less feed pressure so they are particularly suitable for deep cutting in thick material. If the machine is used extensively for rip-sawing then hook-toothed blades are more suitable.

Skip-tooth blades have alternate teeth missing, achieving large gullets without coarse teeth. This makes the skip-tooth blade a good compromise between fast and fine cutting. Thick blades that are wider and stiffer than thin blades are better suited to machines with large diameter wheels that will not over-stress them and shorten their life.

BLADE WIDTH

Narrow blades can cut tightly into curves but wider blades are stiffer and better at resisting sideways flexing, making them most suitable for deep cutting. Narrow blades are less tightly guided by the kerf so they have a tendency to wander. Hence, it is best to choose the width carefully before trying to saw a smooth curve. As a rule of thumb, a blade will cut down to a radius of five times the blade width but this varies with the set of the teeth and width of kerf.

A wider blade is stiffer front to back but it must be properly tensioned. Too much tension can stress the wheel bearings and distort the machine's frame, causing permanent damage. The widest blade that fits on a bandsaw is often too wide for the machine to properly tension. For deep straight cuts such as during re-sawing or cutting veneers or laminates, it is important to hold the blade at full tension. This means using a narrower blade than the maximum for the machine, even though the wider one would be stiffer.

BLADE TENSION

All bandsaw blades need to be under tension to perform well, but wide blades need more tension than narrow ones. Before adjusting the tension, isolate the supply, open the wheel cover doors and slacken off all six blade guides so they are well out of the way. Now you can turn the wheels freely by hand without the guides affecting tracking.

Adjust the tension of the blade by turning the handle or knob that moves the two bandsaw wheels apart. Some machines have a tension gauge that shows high, medium and low tension suitable for different blade widths. Alternatively, you can feel the tension by deflecting a length of blade with your finger and thumb. Some makers pluck the blade like a guitar string and listen for the correct tone. Too much tension and the blade or the machine can be damaged; too little tension and the blade will wander in its kerf.

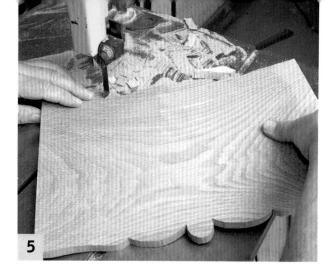

5 For sawing tight curves, use a narrow blade and be prepared to back it off.

6 Use the widest blade possible for long smooth curves.

WHEEL ALIGNMENT

Tracking a bandsaw is a bit like steering a bicycle – very small changes in the alignment of the wheels quickly shift the blade to follow a different course. The wheels must be aligned vertically so they are in the same plane and parallel to each other. Bad wheel alignment will cause the blade to wander around on the wheels, resulting in irregular cuts. This will also reduce the life of the blade, bearings and guides. Use a straightedge and ruler to check the wheels are aligned.

You adjust the tracking by turning a knob, which tilts the arbor (or axle) of the upper wheel, making the blade move backwards or forwards on the rubber tyre. Spin the wheels by hand and adjust the tracking knob until the blade rides centrally on the tyre. On some machines the lower wheel can also be adjusted for tracking, but this is not usually necessary except for major overhaul. Wheel distortion or bearing wear causes the blade tension to vary as the wheel turns – check for this as you inch the wheel round by hand.

GUIDES

Guides are either the roller bearing type or the friction type. Roller bearings run more smoothly when first set up, but accumulate sawdust on the blade rather than scraping it off. Older machines use metal cool-blocks or composite materials for friction guides. Some modern machines have friction guides made from ceramic materials which are extremely hardwearing.

Each time a different blade is fitted, you need to go through a procedure for adjusting the guides. If you consistently use good-quality blades of the same type, you may get away with checking rather than moving the guides after each change.

With the wheels aligned and the blade running true, the guides should be adjusted. Start with the lower back guide and bring it up so it just touches the rear edge of the blade, but does not move it. Bandsaw blades never run perfectly true; there are always small movements due to variations in the shape and stiffness of the material. This means you need to check the adjustment as you turn the wheel by hand. The back of the blade should just touch the back guide – too close and it can cause excessive wear, too far away and the blade will drift in the kerf. Next,

7 Roller bearings grip the blade firmly.

8 The traditional metal 'cool-block' type goes on and on.

set the lower pair of side guides. Move the left guide until it just touches the blade without deflecting it. Now move the right guide in towards the blade. If the guides are friction type, a paper thickness gap is required between the blade and the guide. If the guide is a ball-race type, it can contact the blade. Move the guides forward so their front edges are in line with the base of the tooth gullets. Spin the wheels by hand and make sure the blade does not rub unevenly or jam at the welded joint.

Now lock the lower guides in position and repeat the adjustment procedure for the upper guides, again spinning the wheels by hand to check the blade runs smoothly. Position a square on the table to check that the blade runs through the slot at right angles to the table. If the blade is not truly vertical, adjust the table mounting rather than attempting to correct this by changing the adjustment of the blade guides.

FEEDING TIME

Feed timber into the blade slowly, listening to the sound – it should be smooth and steady, possibly with a tick as the weld passes the guides. If this sound varies it may indicate a kink or crack in the blade.

If the blade cuts consistently to one side rather than following a straight line, it may be because the side guides are loose, allowing the blade to twist to one side. Alternatively there may be uneven set in the teeth, which can happen after running the blade though poorly adjusted guides.

Steadily increase the feed rate, carefully listening and watching to ensure the blade is running straight and smooth. If the sound becomes screeching or the blade wanders, ease off the feed pressure immediately. If the blade does not cut straight it may be that you are using too narrow a blade or cannot achieve the correct tension for that blade. The guides may not be adjusted closely and parallel to the blade or they may be worn. It may also be that your feed rate is too fast. In the long run it is more efficient to cut slowly and accurately, preserving blade life, rather than forcing the timber and producing a rough cut that will need additional planing.

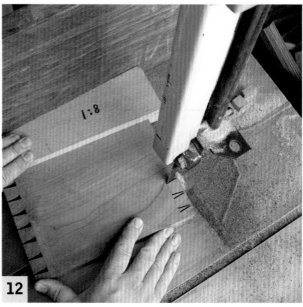

9 The table can be tilted to a measured angle by releasing the clamping bolt beneath.

10 The tilted table allows you to make angled cuts.

11 Neat tenons can be sawn against the bandsaw fence.

12 Using a wedged shim against the bandsaw fence to cut dovetails.

13 Using a wedged platform on the bandsaw table to cut dovetail pins.

14 A wire brush keeps the lower tyre free of sawdust build up.

BANDSAW MAINTENANCE

The guard must be adjusted and doors fitted and locked before restoring power so accidents are avoided and dust collected. Dust extraction from bandsaws is often crude and less effective than from other machines. While the quantity of dust is relatively small, it is fine and potentially hazardous. The lower wheel is normally fitted with an internal brush to keep the tyre clean. This needs routine adjustment for contact with the tyre. Using the bandsaw on softwood will also build up resin deposits on the blade, guides and tyres. Scraping noises within the machine suggest something is severely out of line. This may be due to distortion of the guide post or the machine's frame, or simply a loose offcut in the wheel casing. If a blade comes off the wheel after alignment, it suggests something has worked loose, the tyre has worn out or one of the wheel bearings has failed.

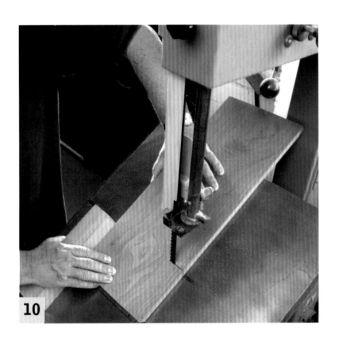

10

11

13

14

Routers and handheld jointing tools

Many power tools on sale are aimed at the DIY market and are not suitable for furniture-makers. However, the router, biscuit, dowel and domino jointers are multifunctional tools that have found their way into many maker's workshops.

Early hand-powered routers were crude grooving planes, consisting of a metal or wooden body with a wide, flat sole and a chisel-like blade poking through and were notoriously awkward to use. Around the middle of the 20th century, electric versions of the router started to be produced. Woodworkers found they could do much more with it than just cutting clean grooves and from that time a whole industry has emerged supplying router cutters and router jigs.

CUTTING GROOVES

The principal job of the modern router is still cutting grooves. With a small cutter set to a shallow depth, it is possible to guide a router by hand for simple pattern carving. For example, using a small

ABOVE This domino jointing tool is a handheld morticer for loose tenons.

1 With the timber clamped flush in a vice the bench top provides a steady base for the router.

V-groove cutter set to a shallow depth, you could sign your name on a piece of timber or carve a motif. However, with a larger diameter straight-sided cutter and the motor turning at the same speed, the cutting edge moves faster. This means it cuts faster, but it also it is harder to control because of the reaction to the cutting force. For that reason, it is not recommended to rout freehand with large cutters and you must have a system to guide the motion. The main options for cutting straight grooves are either to run the router's base against a fence clamped alongside the groove or to use the router's sliding fence to guide the base parallel to the timber's edge.

Looking down on an upright router, the cutter turns clockwise. As you push the cutter from left to right to make a groove, the turning motion tries to force the router away from you. Provided this force pushes the router more firmly against a guide it is not a problem. A suitable guide might be either a piece of wood clamped behind to act as a fence or the router's own sliding fence running against the timber's edge (see drawing). However, if you move the router in the wrong direction, it will be pushed away from the guide and veer off on a course of its own, quite possibly causing damage along the way. This effect, known as snatching, can be quite a problem for those unfamiliar with the tool.

2 It is possible to guide a router by hand for simple pattern carving.

GUIDING A HANDHELD ROUTER TO MAKE A STRAIGHT GROOVE

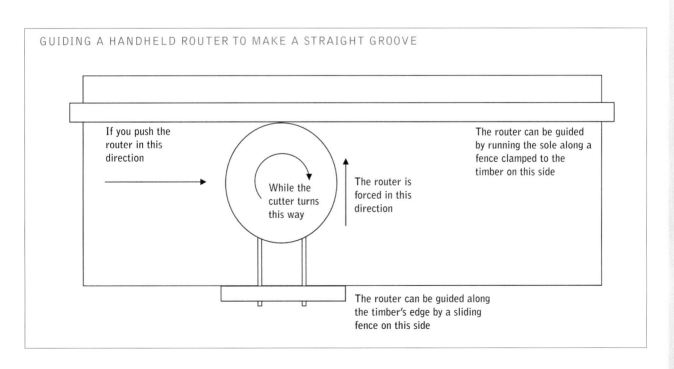

If you push the router in this direction

While the cutter turns this way

The router is forced in this direction

The router can be guided by running the sole along a fence clamped to the timber on this side

The router can be guided along the timber's edge by a sliding fence on this side

DEPTH OF CUT

It is always wise to make a deep groove in several passes with each pass about ⅛–¼in (3–6mm) deeper than the previous one. Routers are fitted with sprung plungers and also a depth stop with a rotating turret to make multiple passes easy and repeatable.

It is often necessary to cut rebates or grooves in the edge of a piece of timber, such as when you are making a frame to go around a panel. The balancing act of running an otherwise unsupported router along a narrow edge is likely to result in a wiggly groove, while the machine teeters from side to side. A good solution is to clamp the timber in a vice flush with the jaws and bench top. That way the whole router base is supported.

BEARING-GUIDED CUTTERS

A straight-sided groove cut with a router will be the full width of the cutter diameter. However, routers are also used for trimming edges, in which case only part of the cutter's width is plunged into the wood. This time you must be careful you move the router in a direction so the turning cutter pushes itself into the wood rather than out of it. If you get this wrong, the router will try to run away from you along the edge of the wood, scarring it but not cutting cleanly.

It is common practice for manufacturers to provide miniature bearings on the ends of cutters to act as guide wheels. With a straight cutter, you can run the bearing along an edge and the cutter will follow it precisely. The bearings may be bolted to the end of cutter and replaced using an Allen key. By fitting smaller bearings, the guided cutter can be used to make accurate rebates.

An alternative to handheld routing, particularly for larger machines with half-inch chucks, is to mount the router on a router table with the cutter uppermost. In this mode it operates like a spindle moulder in miniature with the cutter turning

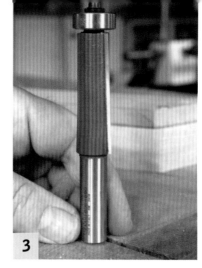

3 A bearing-guided trimmer.

4 Trimming against a template.

5 Small bearings on the end of the cutter enable it to make accurate rebates.

anticlockwise. Using the router table you slide the wood against the router, rather than vice versa. Inverting the router in a table will place the bearing on top. With a template fixed on top of the wood, the cutting edges can be used to duplicate its shape as they trim the wood. Some cutters have bearings that fit over their shaft. These cutters are for use on a router table with a sledge, making them suitable to guide against a template beneath the wood.

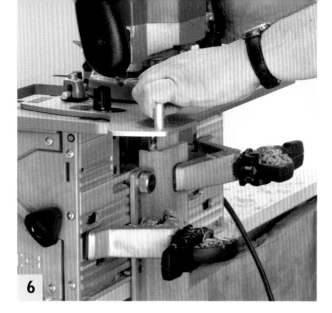

PROFILED EDGES

Before electric routers, cabinetmakers kept huge chests which included many shapes of moulding plane – the router bit has now almost completely replaced these. One router with a case of bits, can now produce chamfers, coves, ogees and ovolos, replacing all these specialist planes. As well as being decorative, profiling bits can be functional, such as panel raisers and matched quadrant cutters used to produce rule joints for folding table tops.

MORTICE AND TENON JIGS

It is possible to make good joints using a router with a straight bit and simple guides. Mortices are simply short, deep grooves with rounded corners. Tenons take more careful setting up and adjustment. More commonly though, people buy router jigs to

6 A mortice and tenon jig.

7 Angling the clamp plate of the mortice and tenon jig.

8 Tenons can be angled in both directions on the mortice and tenon jig.

9 High-speed steel up-cutting bits make tenons with clean shoulders.

perform a task swiftly and with repeatable accuracy. There are now several good mortice and tenon jigs that will enable you to make accurately matched joints. After you have adjusted the jig one for one good fitting joint, producing a set is quick and easy. Straight-sided bits can be used, but up-cutting bits are often preferred. These look like short stubby twist drills with flat ends. They actually work more akin to the cutter of a milling machine which results in very clean edges.

DOVETAIL JIGS

Dovetail jigs for routers use tapered cutters, flared out towards the end to cut sockets and angled sides on the tails. Unlike most other bits, the dovetail cutter needs to work at full depth and make the socket in a single pass so you must move it slowly into the wood. This puts a lot of stress on both the router and the bit so the router needs to be powerful for cutting dovetails and the bit needs to be very sharp.

Simple jigs with comb-pattern templates can produce reliable half-blind dovetails of fixed dimensions, while more sophisticated adjustable jigs will also produce through dovetails of different sizes. Dovetail connoisseurs will notice from the coarser pins that router-cut dovetails do not look as fine as the hand-cut versions; however, they perform just as well and take a fraction of the time, once the jig is set up.

10 Guide bush collars fit behind the fluted bit for dovetail cutting.

11 A dovetail jig with adjustable fingers.

12 Fluted cutters with different sizes and angles for dovetails.

13 Router dovetail jigs make secure joints for boxes and drawers.

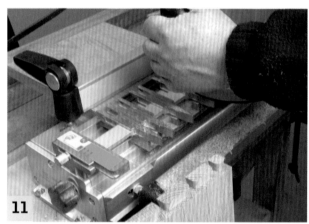

TCT OR HSS BITS

TCT (tungsten carbide tipped) router cutters have a hard material brazed onto the edges of a steel body and this results in a much longer-wearing edge than a steel cutter. TCT cutters are the most common type nowadays but remember that they do have some disadvantages over steel cutters for certain applications. They are more limited in shape so, for example, it would be difficult to make high-performance up-cutters or down-cutters with tungsten carbide tips. You may also find that brand new TCT cutters are not quite as sharp as the best new steel cutters. HSS (or high-speed steel, the high-temperature alloy used for machine tools), will take and hold a very fine edge that tungsten carbide cannot match.

Both TCT and HSS cutters have their uses for different jobs. TCT cutters are good work-horses. They go on cutting long after a steel blade would be blunted. They are resistant to the blunting effect of resin in MDF or plywood but when they are blunt you can only sensibly throw them out. Steel however, can be made very sharp using diamond honing stones and kept that way for fine finishes.

WHEN ROUTERS GO WRONG

All router bits must be securely clamped in the chuck. It is easy to overlook this, especially on an old router where the chuck can be awkward to tighten. The results are disastrous if the cutter breaks loose, but in milder cases the shaft skids in the chuck, causing overheating, while the cutters judder against the timber.

14 Matching cove and ovolo cutters make rule joints for table tops.

15 A router extension gives better access for table work.

16 A large bit hollows out a coving profile against the router table fence.

BISCUIT-JOINTING TOOLS

Biscuits are flat plates that are manufactured from compressed beech wood, designed to fit in a pair of arc-shaped slots, cut with a biscuit jointer. They are designed for jointing at any angle but they are particularly suitable for edge jointing. A biscuit jointer is like a small circular saw that you plunge into the edge of the wood. The tool has a guide frame to control the angle and position of the slot for accurately aligned joints. The biscuiting system is quick and efficient but at $\frac{5}{32}$in (4mm) the biscuits are thin so they need to be used double where strength is required.

17 The biscuit jointer is plunged into an edge.

17

DOWEL-JOINTING TOOLS

A dowel jointer uses a similar adjustable guide frame to a biscuit jointer to align and position a pair of router-type cutting tools. This helps to align and speed up operation when compared to other dowelling systems. Dowels have been used by cabinetmakers for centuries; however, they only offer a small surface for gluing and some makers claim this makes dowel joints more mechanically stressed and prone to failure than others.

DOMINO-JOINTING TOOLS

The newest type of handheld jointing tool at the time of writing is the domino system. This has a router-type cutter in a head that oscillates from side to side, producing a slot mortice. Proprietary loose tenons with rounded edges are sold to fit the slot mortice and these look a bit like domino pieces, hence the name. The advantage of this system is that the tenons are up to 2in (50mm) long so they spread the load deep into the wood. They are up to ⅜in (10mm) thick for strength and they offer a wide flat surface for good long-grain glue adhesion.

USING JOINTING TOOLS

Dowel and domino jointers are used in a similar way to biscuit jointers. You first fit the appropriate cutter and set the cutting depth for the size of biscuit, dowel or domino. Next, offer the two pieces of wood together and pencil-mark the centre line of the joint across both boards (more sophisticated alignment jigs are also available). Position the guide frame so the joint is halfway through the thickness of the wood and the centre line aligned with the pencil-mark on the wood. Clamp the wood and push the motor unit so that the cutter plunges into the wood. Repeat on the other piece of wood. With a glue bottle, line both slots with water-based glue such as PVA that swells the biscuit as well as forming a bond. Press the two halves together and keep them clamped until set.

18

19

18 The domino jointing tool is a versatile handheld slot morticer.

19 Dowels are more suitable for lightly stressed joints.

JARGON BUSTING

biscuit – beech-wood segment pressed in pair of slots to form a rapid joint.
dowel – cylinder of wood pressed in pair of holes for a rapid joint.
domino – rectangular beech-wood block pressed in pair of slot mortices to form a rapid joint.

Laminating

The useful art of laminating, as a method of setting permanent curves in wood, is a flexible technique both in the sense that it is versatile, and that it works with the wood fibre's natural suppleness.

The most commonly seen laminated wooden material is plywood, where alternate layers are bonded with the grain at right angles, to form either flat sheeting or curved products such as stackable chair seats. Here, we will concentrate on a method of laminating that aims to avoid being seen, so as to retain the wood's natural character while giving it a precisely curved shape.

BENDING WOOD

Wood resists bending and, if you push it too far, it will snap. This is particularly true after it has been dried to the low moisture content we use for furniture-making. The reason for this is that wood fibres, although individually pliable, are in tight contact with those alongside them, so they cannot

ABOVE The stiffness of the laminates can be felt by hand-bending before they are glued.

slide over one another. This causes tension in the fibres on the outside of a bend, causing them to be pulled apart by the strain of bending. Three techniques furniture-makers employ to deal with this are:

- Use young, supple wood in the 'green' state and bend it before it dries.
- Steam the wood to soften its fibres, allowing those on the inside of a bend to compress while pulling the piece into shape.
- Cut the wood thinly enough so that there is very little strain on the outside fibres, and the wood will bend without snapping.

Laminating curved shapes takes advantage of the last technique. A piece of wood is sawn into a series of lamina or thin slices, like bacon. Kept in sequence, these are coated in glue and pressed into the desired shape. The glue sets, preventing any slippage between the slices and locking them into a curve. With glue set and the newly shaped component released, each lamination will still have tension trapped in it but, with the outer stretched fibres of one layer bonded to the inner compressed fibres of the next, the finished piece will be stable.

BANDSAW

Ripping through the edge of a board to produce thinner sections is known as re-sawing, and preparing lamina is also a re-sawing operation. A bandsaw is used for this type of work (see pages 84–91 for more information about bandsaws). The thickness of the kerf is narrow, hence there is not too much waste when making a large number of cuts. Depending on the depth capacity of your bandsaw, however, you may only be able to produce narrow laminations.

To cut lamina, you will need a high-sided guide fence on the bandsaw table, standing alongside the blade, separated from it by a gap corresponding to the lamination thickness. The timber is pressed against the fence as well as down on to the table. The normal guide fence supplied with a bandsaw is not tall enough for this purpose, so you will probably need to attach a wooden board to increase its height. Make sure the gap between the fence and

1 A high-sided fence on the bandsaw table is braced to the blade guide.

2 Prepared boards are re-sawn into thin slices or lamina. A chevron mark on the end grain keeps them in sequence.

the blade is even, and there is no significant movement between the two. This may require you to improvise a bracing arrangement to prevent the upper blade guide from moving, relative to the top of the fence.

Use a fresh blade for laminating. Skip-tooth bandsaw blades have extra large gullets between the teeth to carry away waste, making them especially efficient for re-sawing jobs. However, the disadvantage of skip-tooth blades when preparing for lamination is that, although they cut quicker, they leave a rougher surface. With patience, you might manage to slice laminations off hardwoods down to $\frac{1}{16}$in (1.5mm) thickness.

TECHNICAL TIP

Sometimes, if the wood is particularly brittle, steaming the lamina can help soften them before bending and will remove the locked-in tension. Note that steaming also changes the colour of some woods.

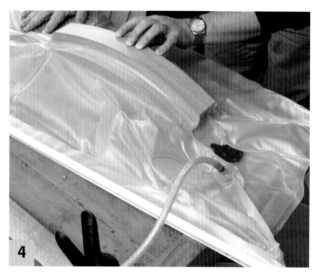

FORMERS

Press laminates into shape while the glue sets between a matching pair of convex and concave moulds or formers, similar to the saddle and caul traditionally used for veneering curved work. You can make cheap and effective formers from MDF, layered up to the required thickness and shaped on the bandsaw. Glue the MDF for repeated use, or just bolt it together for a one-off. The shapes of a pair of curved formers should not exactly match when pressed together, allowing for the thickness of the stack of laminations between them.

Mark the centre line on both formers to help you align them. Also, mark the centre line on the laminations. The formers should be smooth to avoid marking the laminated component, and they can be protected from sticking to glue squeezed out by waxing the inside surfaces.

With glue set and the newly shaped component released, each lamination will still have tension trapped in it, but with the outer stretched fibres of one layer being bonded to the inner compressed fibres of the next, the finished piece should be stable. Inevitably, there will be some relaxation or 'spring-back' when the clamping pressure is removed. Allow for this by exaggerating the curvature of the formers.

3 Two parts to the former are shaped out of MDF.

4 Vacuum bags can be very effective for shaping laminates.

OTHER PRESSES

The band-cramp or strap-clamp is a versatile device consisting of a loop of nylon or canvass webbing, with a tensioning buckle. This can be used to pull a stack of lamina into shape over a single convex former. The vacuum press, primarily designed for veneering, is also very useful for pressing a stack of laminates onto a former of any shape, with even pressure across the surface. By removing air from a vinyl bag with a vacuum pump, the force of atmospheric pressure is applied to the bag and components inside it. The pressure is considerable at 14 pounds per square inch (10 tonnes per square metre), and it acts in every direction. It presses equally hard into the sides of steep curves, whether they are convex or concave. Beware that distortion of the bag is greater when laminating than veneering flat work, so be particularly careful that it is not pulled onto sharp points that may cause damage.

JARGON BUSTING

caul – semi-rigid mould or former used for pressing veneer.

GLUE LINES

The aim is to make the glue lines in laminated work invisible. One way to achieve this is by making the layer of glue, and hence the glue line on the edge, as thin as possible, as this also improves the strength of the bond.

Glue lines show less in coarse-grained woods and the distance between glue lines will vary. Stiff and brittle woods need to be cut thin for bending without steam, typically to $\frac{1}{16}$in (1.5mm) or less, but supple woods like ash and birch can be much thicker, provided the radius is not tight.

GLUING OPTIONS

Spreading glues for laminating needs to be done quickly, due to the large gluing areas – using a paintbrush or foam roller. A long open time is desirable when you are trying to keep the pieces aligned. Chemical reactions speed up with heat, so if the workshop is warm, prepare well for gluing.

Formaldehyde-based synthetic resins are supplied as powder to which you add water and mix to a paste. Spread it across the laminations with a brush or roller. You can add water-based stains while mixing to bring the colour closer to that of the wood. Two-part epoxy resins are a good choice as they have gap-filling ability, and do not swell the wood locally by releasing moisture into it. Polyurethane glues do not add water but actually extract moisture from the air and wood in the chemical reaction that results in setting – this can cause thin veneers to buckle due to over-drying.

PVA glues are not suitable for gap filling and allow some creep when set but they can be used successfully for laminating, provided the lamination surfaces are flat, so they sit together with no gaps.

FINISHES

Finishing a laminated edge can cause problems because the absorption of surface finishes by the glue lines will generally be less than by the wood. Make a trial laminate to test out every stage of the process and the behaviour of surface finishes.

The mechanical behaviour of a laminated component will be similar to a straight piece of the same cross-section but laminated parts are not good for external use. Even if fully waterproof glue is used, the layer of glue will act as a moisture barrier so the wood movement on one side of the glue line will be different from that on the other. The force on the glue will generally be irresistible and result in delamination. If a laminated piece is to be exposed to extremes of humidity, use a sealed finish to slow moisture transmission in the outer layers.

5 Two parts of the former are cramped together.

6 In the wet, different wood movement each side of the glue layer causes delaminating.

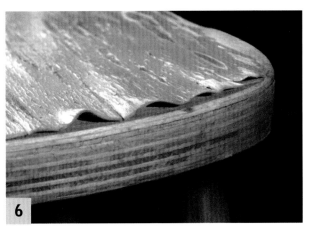

Bandsawn veneers

Bandsawn veneers offer new dimensions to your work as a furniture-maker. The figuring of the wood – the patterns where fibres meet the surface – can follow any direction you choose, while end grain and joints need not be visible at all.

Solid-wood furniture must conform to certain construction principles in order to prevent clashes in wood movement. The designs are always ruled by the functional limitations of wood movement determining grain direction. However, the ground material or substrate chosen for a piece of veneered furniture can be selected for stability, placing no such constraints on the outward appearance.

WHY VENEER?

If veneered furniture is so much more versatile than solid-wood construction, you may ask why it is not used more often by furniture-makers? One of the reasons is the greater effort and cost involved in the additional processes of veneering. Another reason is that many people are charmed by the 'what you see

ABOVE Pulling timber through a bandsaw with a cork pressure pad.

1 Bandsawn veneers are thick enough to handle without them curling.

is what you get' character of solid-wood furniture. In Victorian times, veneer was sometimes used as a mask for bad workmanship sold to clients with little understanding of quality. However, veneering is used today by many of the makers at the very top end of the furniture market. For these makers, there is no question about the quality of their work and hence there is no need to put their construction techniques on display.

PREPARE THE BANDSAW

Unplug the bandsaw before making any adjustments. Clean up the internals and blade contact surfaces with a brass wire brush, but do not use one with steel bristles, as it will cause scratching or damage. The fences supplied with bandsaws are invariably too low for cutting veneer against, and must be raised with a supplementary fence. The ideal for this is a thick, square-edged block of hardwood or plywood screwed to the front of the standard fence. The square edge ensures the fence stands vertically on the table, while the thickness prevents it bowing or vibrating. If you can, arrange to fit an additional stay between the top of the fence and the upper blade guide. A long bolt or piece of threaded rod is usually best for this

2 A high-sided wooden fence is fitted onto the bandsaw table.

– it will act as a stabilizing bracket and ensure that the veneer is cut to a uniform thickness, which needs to be maintained constant.

FRESH BLADES

For deep cutting into hardwoods, fresh bandsaw blades are essential. Old, blunt teeth would not only cut slowly with potential for burning, but they would also require extra pressure, making them likely to veer off to the side. For deep rip sawing into hardwoods, skip-tooth blades with $\frac{5}{16}$in (8mm) pitch (3 teeth per inch) are preferred. The large gullets between the teeth carry away the dust accumulated by the long travel of each tooth.

GUIDES

Bandsaw blade guides consist of either roller bearings, which are the most common type, or cool-blocks, which are fixed friction bearings designed to conduct heat away. In either case, they need particularly careful adjustment before attempting to cut veneers. The advantage of roller bearings over blocks is that they can be adjusted for tighter contact, without excessive friction, making them more effective at preventing the blade from twisting – particularly important while you are slicing off a thin veneer.

The disadvantage is that while blocks scrape surface deposits off the blade, keeping it clean, bearings compress sawdust onto the blade, building up a residue and requiring extra diligence with a brass wire brush to remove. With the upper and lower sets of guides slackened off so that they do not interfere with blade movement, the bandsaw wheels may need to be adjusted by tilting, so the

3

TECHNICAL TIP

While the ideal bandsaw for deep ripping would have a wide blade pulled to maximum tension, this is rarely achievable in practice because of the strain it places on the machine's frame, pulling the blade away from true vertical.

I recommend fitting a narrower than maximum blade, so that the machine will take full tension, without any distortion. Fit a new blade before cutting veneer, then adjust the tension to the maximum for the blade and the machine.

4

5

blade runs centrally on the tyres when the wheels are test-spun by hand. The rear guides can then be adjusted forward so that they just touch the back of the blade. The side bearings are then adjusted forwards so they pinch the blade just behind the tooth gullets. The side pressure from rollers should be enough to prevent sideways movement in the mouth, but they should not grip so tightly that the rollers cannot be turned without the blade moving. Cool-block guides need a paper thickness clearance so they are tight enough to prevent any significant sideways movement, but should not jam the band anywhere, particularly at the welded joint.

THICKNESS CONTROL

Like other saws, bandsaw blades have teeth that are set or angled to either side, so they cut a kerf with extra thickness to prevent jamming. When you measure the distance between the blade and the fence, it is important to find the innermost teeth,

3 The guides just pinch the blade with no slop.

4 Adjust the rear guides so the back of the blade just touches, and move the side guides forward to just behind the teeth.

5 There should not be enough pressure to prevent the guides skidding on the blade.

as these are the ones that control the thickness. The distance between blade and fence must be the same top and bottom, so if you have fitted a stabilizing bracket on the fence it will need careful adjustment.

SLICING THE TIMBER

Face and edge plane a board of dried timber, just as you would do when working with solid wood. Press the board against the high fence as you feed it into the blade. Patience is essential when sawing veneers. Don't forget that while the piece you are removing may be very thin, the bandsaw blade is sawing through a depth of typically 8in (200mm). Listen to the blade as it slowly slices into the timber and feel the light pressure it takes to keep the kerf going. Do not force it as this will send it off course.

Use pressure pads – these can be simply cork sanding blocks – so if the blade did break through the surface, it won't cause injury. When you are more than halfway through each cut, move around to the outfeed side of the bandsaw table and pull the remainder of the board through the saw. Bandsawn veneers are typically between $\frac{1}{16}$ and $\frac{1}{8}$in (1.5 and 3mm) thick, so they do not offer the same immunity to movement as knife-cut commercial veneers, where the thickness is typically not much more than $\frac{1}{40}$in (0.6mm).

GLUING BANDSAWN VENEER

Each piece of veneer will have a sawn face, which is tooth-marked but smooth enough to glue directly, and a smooth surface, which was planed before being pressed against the fence during sawing. When face veneers are glued onto a substrate, a backing veneer of the same thickness and similar properties is glued on to the other side. This has the function of equalizing the stresses caused by the initial drying and seasonal movement of the face veneer. It also gives the reverse side a consistent look.

VENEER PRESSES

The veneer must be pressed in place while the glue sets. For small surfaces, the pressure can be made with cramps or a mechanical press, but for larger areas, it requires a massive steel frame. Air press benches use air pressure to apply the force. By placing an object beneath a flexible sheet, then extracting the air from beneath the sheet with a vacuum pump, enormous pressure acts uniformly on the object. Vacuum presses have become more practical for the small workshop. These comprise of a small electric pump and a vinyl bag with sealable ends, to be laid out on a flat bench.

6 With firm pressure against the fence, feed the timber steadily into the blade.

7 Veneers are sawn and trimmed before being glued on a substrate.

8 Pressure while the glue sets comes from a vacuum bag.

Angles on chair curves

The curves and angled joints involved in making chairs can be a time-consuming and daunting process which puts many makers off. However, these essential techniques will help you to tackle this specialist area with confidence.

Chair frames need curved components and angled joints. You might make a simple chair with the legs and the seat rails all straight and joined at right angles, but even then the back must be raked at an angle to prevent an awkward forward-leaning position for the sitter.

Mass-produced chairs are astonishingly cheap because of the economies of scale provided by jigs and CNC machines as well as replicating large numbers of parts from bulk materials. One-off chairs take a disproportionate amount of effort to make and for this reason chair-making tends to be treated as a specialist area that some bespoke furniture designer-makers avoid. However, producing chairs in small batches, such as for a dining set, can also provide some benefits of scale to the individual maker.

ABOVE A spokeshave is the perfect tool for cutting chamfers to prevent splinters forming on curved edges. This keeps them friendly to the touch and provides a light-catching visual detail.

TECHNICAL TIP

No other rigid artefact makes such close contact with the body as a chair, yet many mass-produced examples are anything but a good fit. If a chair is to be comfortable, its shape must take account of the human form. The design process is often an evolutionary one with the maker building on previous successes and also learning from previous problems.

TEMPLATES FOR CHAIRS

A 'rod' is a full-sized drawing marked out on a board, allowing the shapes of components and the angle of fit between them to be checked out. The shapes can then be transferred to another board for cutting out as templates. MDF or plywood are the most suitable materials of rods and templates. Using rods and templates allows the makers to repeat the shapes of previously made components and improve on them over time.

Templates also ensure that matching parts of a chair, or a set of chairs, are the same shape. Makers build up sets of templates over the years, sometimes mixing components between sets to produce alternative designs and often varying the shape to derive new template designs.

MARKING OUT

Components are marked on the stock timber around the template using a pencil or felt-tip pen ready for cutting on the bandsaw. It takes considerable time and care to coordinate the shapes with the direction of grain, both for aesthetic appeal and to ensure there is no risk of short-grain failure at points of high stress, such as around the rear leg joints.

Curved components are often 'nested' so that one is cut from inside another to avoid excess wastage. While the unusually shaped offcuts are inevitably numerous, it is often possible to mark chair components around faults or unwanted features such as knots in the wood in a way that may not be possible with rectangular furniture. All this takes time and the more complex the chair is, the longer it will take to mark the shapes and cut the parts.

1 Templates are shaped for each component.

2 Marking around the template onto the wood.

BANDSAWN CHAIR PARTS

The bandsaw is an invaluable machine for cutting out the shaped components of chairs (see pages 84–91 for more information about bandsaws). Tenons for sturdy joints can also be cut on the bandsaw as part of the same process. A narrow blade is necessary for negotiating tight curves; as a rule of thumb the tightest curve you can cut has a radius of five times the blade width. In practice this depends on how much set has been applied to the teeth and hence how wide the kerf is.

It is best to cut curves slowly with the kerf just meeting the outside edge of the line so as to minimize the excess to be trimmed off later. At the same time, the kerf should not cross the line otherwise there will be a blemish to remove when the component is trimmed.

If a component is to be shaped on the bandsaw in two axes, it is essential to support the underside, normally by using the first offcut during the second cut. This will avoid the snatching that can occur if a poorly supported piece of wood becomes trapped by the blade. While bandsaws are normally benign, even-tempered machines, it can be surprising how aggressive they become if poorly supported wood is allowed to snatch and jar against the momentum of the wheels.

3

TRIMMING TO SIZE

Router cutters fitted with guide bearings above or below can be used to trim curved components to match the exact outline of the template. The template is clamped against the rough-sawn component, which is very slightly larger because it was bandsawn to the outside edge of the line. The work is normally done on a heavy-duty router table or spindle moulder while the component and template are clamped to a sliding carriage or 'sledge'. The cutter height is arranged so it runs

4

3 Bandsawing out a marked component.

4 Before cutting curves in a second dimension the component is taped to the offcut.

5 For use on the router table, cutters have guide bearings above or below.

6 The guide bearing bears against the template while the component is clamped to a sledge.

7 A compass plane fairs curves to a constant radius.

8 Old wooden spokeshaves are very controllable for curved edge work.

along the component while the bearing runs along the template. Much care must be taken to avoid snatching at the start of a cut, generally by making the template longer than the component.

For hand-tool work, the compass plane has the same mechanism as a normal Bailey plane but the sole is made from a flexible steel strip, held in a curve by a large control screw. Having produced a rough-sawn shaped component on the bandsaw you need to fair the curves smooth so hands can glide over them and clothes will not catch.

The compass plane is an ideal tool for this, provided the radius of the sawn curve is large and constant. If the radius varies, you can plane it in small sections, adjusting the curvature as you move along. Traditional tool users also find that old wooden spokeshaves, when tuned-up, are very controllable and well suited to curved edge work. The relatively wide mouth and steep cutting angle of the forged blade work surprisingly well inside tight curves, and changes of radius are no problem.

5

6

7

8

JARGON BUSTING

sledge – sliding carriage on machine table to carry wood over blades.

rotary carver – a disk with chainsaw-type teeth, powered by an angle-grinder motor.

BULK REMOVAL

Where large quantities of material need to be hollowed out, such as for producing shaped wooden seat tops, the rotary carver is a fairly aggressive woodcutting tool that can, with practice, be controlled to produce neat work. The device is in effect a steel disc edged with chainsaw teeth that is fitted to an angle-grinder. It is provided with a guard that also limits the depth of cut, but for more precise work you need to provide further means of regulating it.

Disc sanders are also used by some chair-makers, while others look on them with disapproval as tools of the motor-repair shop. However, they are easily controlled and quickly remove material on components or assembled chairs. Some well-regarded makers assemble chairs to quite a rough form, and then produce most of the detailed shaping after the frame is glued up.

MARKING ANGLED JOINTS

Chair joints are like any other furniture joint in principle but there are two specific factors to consider. Firstly, the joints often meet at an angle and, secondly, they need to be particularly strong. The main joints between legs and seat rails can be severely stressed, especially if heavy sitters rock in their chairs or shuffle around in them, racking the joints. Chair legs and frames need to be exceptionally well fitted, making best use of the component's dimensions.

Before cutting an angled joint, it is necessary to measure the angle and position or transfer this information onto the component. This can be done by clamping the components in alignment before knife-marking the shoulder lines; however, when the joints are angled in two dimensions, direct marking becomes particularly difficult. It is not possible to align the shoulders of the uncut component in the way you would do with conventional furniture. Small protractor gauges

9

10

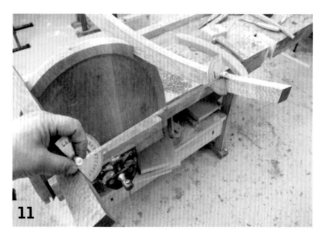

11

are useful for transferring lengths and angles. I have joined two of these together at the stems to make a double-ended instrument that I often use for marking the joints on rails.

9 Bulk material can be removed from a seat with a rotary carver.

10 Compound angled rail joints can be positioned with the style joints disengaged.

11 A double-ended angle gauge is valuable for measuring rail joint angles.

ANGLED JOINTING JIGS

In the past, dowels were used on mass-produced chairs because they are relatively easy to fit in the angled ends of components. However, dowel joints frequently fail in end grain by breaking out of the side when they are subjected to heavy loading such as in seat-rail joints. Small loose-fitted tenons have similar limitations. Large-diameter dowels can be turned on a lathe and used effectively as large-section loose tenons for heavy-duty joints.

Mortice and tenon joints can be cut at an angle either by hand or on the bandsaw, or by using a router together with a frame mortice and tenon jig. These jigs allow either the mortice, or more usefully the tenon, to be cut at a controlled angle. You can also cut tenons at a compound angle by sloping both the timber and the jig's clamping plate.

PULLING CHAIRS TOGETHER

The chair is usually glued up in stages, such as the back frame followed by the front then the side rails. Sash cramps are not very effective because they apply forces at right angles to the rails and they are also heavy. Lightweight cramps can be successful on small components such as back rails if the joints are near to right-angled. However, band-cramps are ideal for pulling together chair frames. They are light and pull joints at any angle while not imposing a distorted shape on the seat.

FINISHING CHAIRS

Chairs are designed for touching – so they need to feel good to the fingertips. The surface must be smooth and free from sharp edges, while the finish must be stable. Chamfered edges help provide a smooth finish where any two surfaces meet at an arris and they are particularly valuable on the edges of curved components. This is because there is always a point on the curve where it would be prone to forming a splinter if it were left as a sharp edge, and the chamfer takes away this tendency.

12 Frame mortice and tenon jigs for routers are valuable chair-making tools.

13 Curved components can be tenoned on the jig.

14 Band-cramps are ideal for pulling together angled frames.

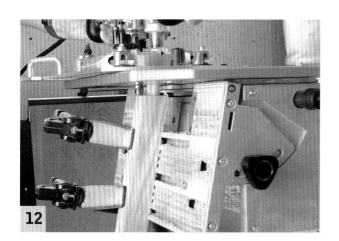

12

13

14

Part Two Projects

Oak stool

 Skill level 1 |  Hand tools

This simple, but attractive, rustic-style oak stool puts into practice some basic bridle (see page 47) and edge jointing (see page 40). The design is versatile and can be adapted as your confidence grows.

ABOVE The finished stool.

Although this stool is straightforward, the design could be adapted for many purposes. For example, by varying the dimensions, the design could either be stretched longways to make a coffee table or upwards to create a hallstand. Oak (*Quercus robur*) is good for cutting simple joints like these because it is strong and it splits easily along the grain. Chestnut (*Castanea dentata*) or ash (*Fraxinus excelsior*) will behave in similar ways. Imported oak is usually more straight-grained and evenly coloured than British oak, as well as being more readily available, so it gives tidier results but, arguably, it has less character.

TIMBER PREPARATION

Before working wood that has been dried, it should be stored in a place with a similar atmospheric moisture range to where the furniture will be used. If you plan to keep the stool near a radiator, store the timber near one. That way, any changes of shape will have taken place before you cut the final dimensions and the stool will not pull itself apart.

After removing any cracked ends from the timber, start by measuring and marking out the four legs and the five rails from 1½in (38mm) stock. Cut this to a square section then plane the reference face on it. The legs and the rails for this project are all made from material of the same cross-section.

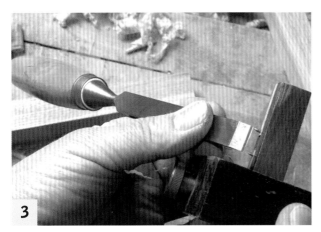

Use a marking gauge, with its stock pressed against the reference face to mark the thickness of the planed components to 1¼in (32mm). Use a try square to set the other two surfaces at right angles. Angling the plane while smoothing is better for shearing awkward grain and, by varying the angle, you can avoid tearing. Bear in mind that angling also reduces the plane's effective length. This means that the guaranteed straightness of the surface also reduces, so while this technique is acceptable for short legs and rails, it is no use while edge jointing, when maximum straightness is required.

CUTTING LIST

- 1 x seat top: oak (edge-jointed)
  13 x 13 x 1in (325 x 325 x 25mm)
- 4 x off legs: oak
  20 x 1¼ x 1¼in (500 x 32 x 32mm)
- 5 x off rails: oak
  12 x 1¼ x 1¼in (300 x 32 x 32mm)

1 Four legs and five rails are cut and planed from square-section oak.

2 The width of a joint is marked directly from the corresponding piece.

3 The mortice gauge is set to width against a chisel.

4 The same gauge settings are used for the pins and sockets of the bridle joint.

MARKING JOINTS

The bridle joint is a type of mortice and tenon (see page 47). The marking consists of the knifed shoulder line that runs around the timber and the gauged lines for the cheeks that run along and across the end. The lines are marked in the same positions for both the peg and the socket.

The width of a joint is marked directly from the corresponding piece with a knife line to show where the shoulders and the socket base will be. Make a nick in the wood to mark the position, and then insert the knife tip in the nick and slide a try

Components and measurements of the oak stool

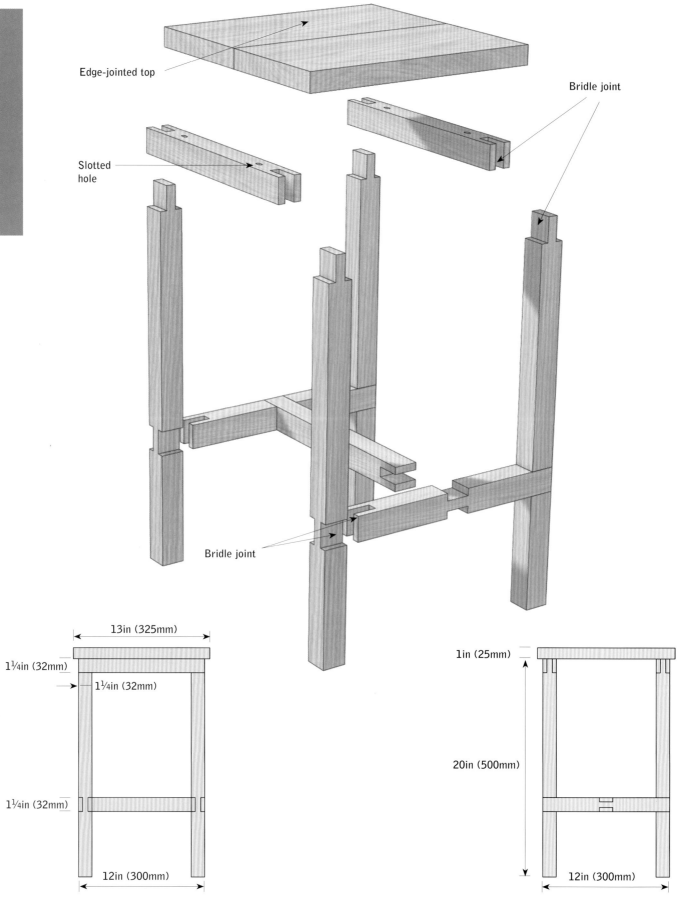

Edge-jointed top

Slotted hole

Bridle joint

Bridle joint

13in (325mm)

1¼in (32mm)

1¼in (32mm)

1¼in (32mm)

12in (300mm)

1in (25mm)

20in (500mm)

12in (300mm)

5 For sawing the sockets, the kerf runs on the inside edge of the gauge line.

6 The socket base is chopped out with V-shaped chippings.

7 The shoulders of the pin are sawn with the kerf on the outside edge of the line.

8 Sockets for T-shaped bridle joints are chopped with a broad chisel across the grain.

9 The socket bases are pared flat with a fine chisel.

square up against the knife before running the blade along the square's edge to make the line. A mortice gauge with two marking spurs is handy for this type of joint because you can set the width and the position of the mortice independently. The same gauge settings are used for the pins and sockets of the bridle joint.

The lines of the cheeks divide the thickness of the wood into three, so the peg will be one-third of the width and the two sides of the socket will form the other two-thirds. For improved strength, I chose to increase the thickness of the peg slightly to ½in (12.7mm), which also corresponds to a standard chisel size, handy for chopping out the socket.

The joint is placed in the centre of the wood. It is important to note here that the stock is pressed against the corresponding faces of both pieces forming the joint. That way, if the positioning of the joint happens to be slightly off-centre, it will still fit without creating stepped surfaces.

CUTTING JOINTS

With the marking lines in the same position for the peg and socket, the saw cut, or kerf, must always run along the waste side of the line. For the socket cheeks, this means the kerf is inside the line, while for the cheeks of the pegs the kerf is outside the line.

Rather than a bevel-edged chisel, use a square-sided type to chop out the base of the socket so it does not have delicate corners that would be easily damaged and so that its sides register between the cheeks, holding it square. The socket bases are chopped out with a succession of V-shaped chippings, keeping the base closely inside the line. This allows you to pare away the final slice for a crisp undented edge.

The T-shaped bridle joints have the same design of socket but the pins are formed partway along the legs where the timber must be reduced in section. Make saw cuts down to the gauge lines, keeping the saw level so it just meets the line on each side.

With the wood securely clamped, the waste is chopped across the grain using a broad chisel. As the recess approaches the gauge line, make finer and finer chops, finally paring halfway across the base of the recess. Turn the wood around and pare from the other side, then turn it over to saw and chop out the recess from the opposite face.

FITTING JOINTS

The stool frame is first assembled as two H-frame shapes, formed by a pair of legs and a side stretcher between them. Once they are glued and set, the top rails then join the H-frames and the central cross stretcher to become an A-shaped frame when viewed from the side.

All the joints are dry-fitted without using glue, to test them. You should aim for joints that fit directly from the saw cut, the main reason being that it drastically reduces the time taken and helps you get projects finished. Do not force tight joints together as this will either split the wood immediately or trap in stress so the wood splits later. Paring away the cheeks and shoulders of a tight joint can still give first-class results, but it requires great care and patience as well as a very sharp chisel.

PVA glue is brushed into the sockets so that when the pin is inserted, glue is pushed into the joint. If you were to glue the surface of the pin, this would be scraped off as it was inserted into the socket, resulting in a dry joint and a messy surface outside.

Use a flat reference surface for assembly of the components and frames and a large try square or roofer's square to check the joints are right-angled. Make sure no glue dribbles onto your reference surface, or wipe it off immediately if this happens. Small beads of glue exuding from the closed joint can be left to chisel off when set, in preference to rubbing them into the wood's surface.

When the joints are thoroughly set, clamp the frame in a vice and, using a finely set smoothing plane with a razor-sharp blade, shave across the

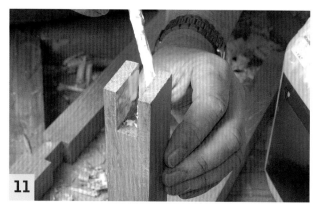

10 The joints are trial fitted to be firmly hand tight.

11 PVA glue is brushed into the sockets.

12 The frame is laid on a flat surface while the glue sets.

joints to bring the surfaces flush. Do not shave off the edge of a frame that includes end grain unless you have chamfered this first. Planing across joints on a finished frame can be challenging because of the differing grain directions, but it will show your finished joints at their best.

SEAT TOP

The top is a square board made by butt or edge jointing two pieces together (see also page 40). If the boards are quarter-sawn (looking at the end grain the annual growth rings are at right angles to

the face) they will stay flat. Otherwise, arrange the boards so the growth rings curve in opposite directions. That way any subsequent cupping of the two halves will tend to cancel.

With the boards clamped face-to-face in a vice, plane both edges together ready for jointing. Check that the edges meet accurately by flipping one board over and standing it edge-to-edge with a bright light behind. Any glimmer between the edges means further planing is needed. If gaps are forming, this means the plane is rocking lengthways and more care is needed to press on the front knob at the start of each stroke and the rear tote or handle at the end of the stroke. When no light is visible, the two sides of the top can be glued.

ATTACHING THE TOP

When a flat top is fixed to a frame, there is often a conflict of grain direction with potential for stress to the frame or splitting of the top. One of the simplest ways to deal with this is to screw the top through slotted holes in the frame. The slots in the upper rails of the frame run at right angles to the direction of the grain in the top. Allow for a 3% movement in the wood so, if the screws are 8in (200mm) apart, make the slots ¼in (6mm) wider

13 Two halves of the top are planed together.

14 The edge joint is glued on one surface for clamping.

15 The frame is screwed onto the top through elongated holes.

16 A simple beeswax finish is traditional for oak.

than the screws. The screws are waxed and fully tightened, then released slightly to allow movement in the slot if tension arises.

FINISHED STOOL

A microbevel shaved with a block plane can be used to avoid leaving a delicate sharp edge or arris that can easily splinter.

Beeswax finish is one of the quickest and simplest ways to provide oak furniture with a lasting warm glow. It will repel dirt and create a silky surface which, while not durable, is easily maintained and improves with age. Either use a proprietary beeswax paste, or you can apply pure beeswax without solvents if you warm the wooden surface using a hot-air gun. Rub the block of wax against the wood and as it turns to liquid, allow some seconds for it to soak in, then wipe away the excess. Ensure there are no solidified dribbles left, then rub the surface with a fresh cotton rag.

Elm cabinet

 Skill level 1 | Hand tools

This cabinet is a development of the frame for the stool in project 1. The main difference is that, instead of bridle joints, this frame uses haunched mortice and tenons (see page 48), and a carcass dovetail (see page 54) for the top rail.

ABOVE The finished cabinet.

Mortice and tenon joints fix the frame and panel construction of this low cabinet, a simple technique, proven over centuries on cabinets of all shapes and sizes. This project uses some specialized planes and spokeshaves for shaping edges.

Vertical stiles and horizontal rails are jointed together in a framework, grooved on their inside edges. The panels are trapped in these grooves to form the back and sides of the cabinet, during the stage when the frame joints are brought together and glued. Clearance between the edge of the panel and bottom of the groove allows the panel to expand and contract. Doorframes on the front have similar panels trapped in grooves. This system overcomes the problems of wide, solid timber forcing the joints apart, while the wood changes size and shape with seasonal humidity changes – particularly relevant in our modern centrally heated homes.

THE WOOD

Elm, with its knotty figuring and wild grain patterns, is ideal for this traditional construction project. It also helps give it a timeless appearance so it is not likely to be discarded as a whim of future fashion. You can still find elm boards that are not too expensive from specialist timber suppliers, such as tree surgeons who fell locally and convert for drying. Elms are likely to be victims of Dutch elm disease which attacks the bark, killing the tree, but does not damage the heartwood. There are many varieties of elms and they form hybrids so, unless pieces come from the same tree, they are unlikely to match. Choose pieces carefully and even if the frame and panel woods do not match, you can balance the colour and grain patterns. For stability, the frames should be chosen from straight-grained wood while the panels trapped in them need not be. Elm dust is irritating to the respiratory system so you need protection if machining it, but with

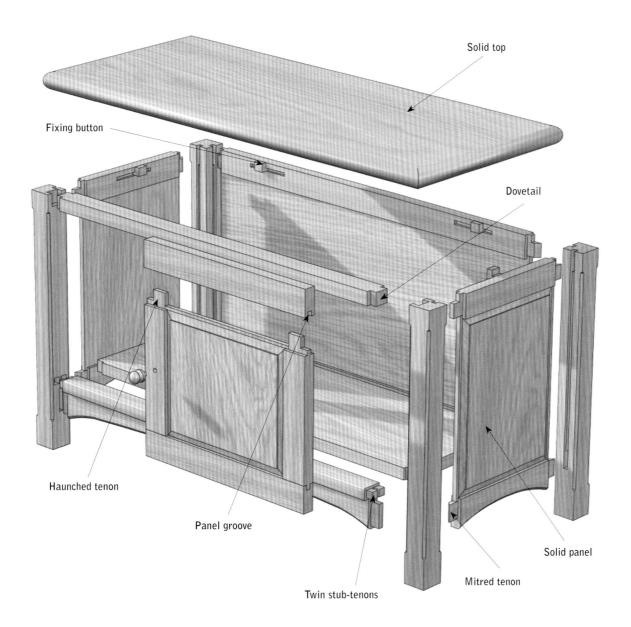

Solid top

Fixing button

Dovetail

Haunched tenon

Panel groove

Twin stub-tenons

Mitred tenon

Solid panel

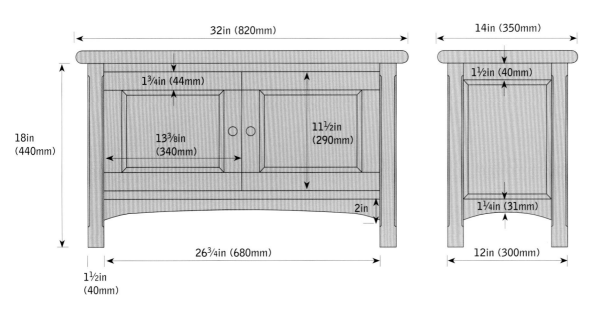

32in (820mm)

14in (350mm)

1³⁄₄in (44mm)

1¹⁄₂in (40mm)

18in
(440mm)

13³⁄₈in
(340mm)

11¹⁄₂in
(290mm)

1¹⁄₄in (31mm)

2in

26³⁄₄in (680mm)

12in (300mm)

1¹⁄₂in
(40mm)

CUTTING LIST

- 1 x seat top: elm (edge-jointed)
  32 x 14 x 1¼in (820 x 350 x 32mm)
- 4 x off legs: elm
  18 x 1½ x 1½in (440 x 40 x 40mm)
- 4 x off carcass rails: elm
  29 x 1½ x 1¼in (730 x 40 x 32mm)
- 1 x off carcass sub rail: elm
  29 x 2 x 1in (730 x 50 x 25mm)
- 4 x off carcass end rails: elm
  11 x 1½ x 1¼in (275 x 40 x 32mm)
- 4 x off door rails: elm
  13½ x 1¾ x 1in (340 x 44 x 25mm)
- 4 x off door stiles: elm
  11½ x 1¾ x 1in (290 x 44 x 25mm)
- 2 x off door panels: elm
  11¼ x 9 x 1in (282 x 227 x 25mm)
- 4 x off top fixing buttons: elm
  2 x 1½ x 1½in (50 x 40 x 40mm)
- 1 x back panel: cedar
  28 x 12 x ¾in (700 x 300 x 18mm)
- 1 x base panel: cedar
  28 x 12 x ¾in (700 x 300 x 18mm)

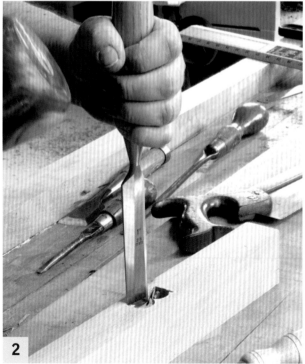

hand-tool work, this is not a problem. It is always best to leave kiln-dried wood in the workshop for a couple of weeks to make sure it has settled, but in the case of elm, I would extend this to a couple of months. Oak, chestnut, or ash would be suitable alternatives for a cabinet like this, and they are better behaved than elm with regard to wood movement. Using frame and panel construction, there should be no problems with any species.

FRAMEWORK

If you are going to make a space beneath a cabinet, it is best to provide enough room to allow cleaning and retrieval of lost items. The arched opening produced by the shaped lower rail would also provides a useful cubbyhole. If you can, choose a piece of elm with curved grain to match the shape

1 To speed up the morticing process, use a Forstner drill to remove waste.

2 Chop the mortices square with a chisel.

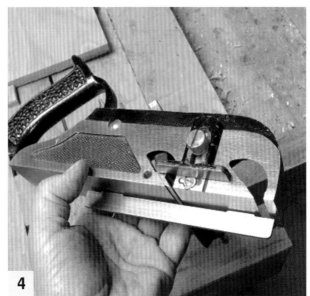

of the arch. The extra depth at the ends of this bottom rail helps to brace the corner posts and stiffen the structure.

Saw the four legs or corner posts of the cabinet from a single 1⅝in (40mm) thick board to ensure even colour and patterning. Rip-saw the fronts of the two front posts from each other so that the grain patterns are book-matched. After facing and edging the timber to make it flat and square-sided, you need to cut mortices to receive the rails and matching tenons. Allow extra height in the corner posts for 'horns' to be sawn off once the joints are glued and set.

The frame is fixed together by haunched mortice and tenon joints at the top. The top rails are lap dovetailed into the corner posts. The front and back of the cabinet are made to a similar layout, except that the rear has a pair of 2in (50mm) deep rails. The front has a 1in (25mm) deep upper and lower door rail, with a concave support beneath the lower rail. The bottom ends of the corner posts are chamfered at the feet, which could otherwise splinter or catch on carpets. All the other edges have stopped chamfers, the bulk removed with a spokeshave then ended with a 45° chisel cut.

FIELDED PANELS

A panel must be reduced in thickness at the edge to allow it to fit into the grooves. This is done by planing away the edge, or fielding it. There are various designs of fielding, but one of the simplest and most effective is a very shallow-angled bevel that wedges lightly into the groove, while still permitting small changes in panel width.

A good tool for cutting the fielding is a rebate plane. This is an open-sided plane with a built-in guide fence and a vertical spur-blade or 'nicker' at the side, especially good for slicing across end grain without causing tear-out. With practice, you can hold the plane at a constant shallow angle to chamfer an edge, and the nicker will follow the same line on each pass. The thickness of the fielded edge must be carefully checked, and a grooved rail offered up to it to ensure a snug fit.

3 Chamfering edges on the corner posts with a spokeshave.

4 An open-sided rebate plane with the vertical 'nicker' blade to slice through end grain and define an edge to the rebate.

5

6

The object of frame and panel construction is to allow the panel to float inside the grooved frame but furniture-makers often glue the panel in the groove at a couple of points to prevent it from rattling. If it is only glued on a short length of the centre of each end-grain field, this will not prevent the panel expanding and contracting. Alternatively, an open-sided rebate can be cut inside the frames, and a moulding used to hold the panel in place.

5 Fielding a panel using a rebate plane.

6 A plough plane or multiplane cuts the rebates to accept fielded panel edges.

7 A brass screw forms a pivot pin, fitting in either a brass plate or a stack of washers.

8 Washers define the clearance above and below the door to prevent it jamming.

BOOK-MATCHING

If you choose the door panels and the frame material from consecutive planks and arrange them carefully, they can have book-matched figuring – in other words, each panel looks like a mirror image of the other. In practice, by the time you have planed each board, the patterns will differ a little, but the effect still looks pleasing and coordinated. You can buy door handles but if you have access to a lathe, they are simple enough to turn. Burr elm is ideal for contrast and coordination with this cabinet.

HINGES

This cabinet avoids metal hinges by the use of concealed pivot pins. As well as making the hinging practically invisible, these pins are easy to fit, and they wear well. The doors are planed to fit their openings snugly. At this stage, it is best to leave them a little tight, as long as they fit in the opening without force, so you can adjust them later.

The pins are made from large brass screws with their plain shafts rotating in brass washers. The washers are trapped in counter-bored holes in the frame. Alternatively, as I did, you can cut a rectangular plate for the shaft to pivot in instead of washers. A small pilot hole is drilled through the upper and lower carcass rail in the hinge position, 1in (25mm) from the carcass side and halfway through the door thickness. With the door wedged in position, a needle is pushed through each pilot hole to mark the door edge. The pilot hole can now be enlarged partway through to fit the washers, and the remainder to fit the pivot screw.

The doorframe is then drilled and the parts trial assembled. If all is well, the frame can be removed, planed to a clearance, and then refitted. The doors must have bevelled edges so they clear the cabinet frame and swing freely through an angle of about 120°, giving excellent access inside the cabinet. It is

7

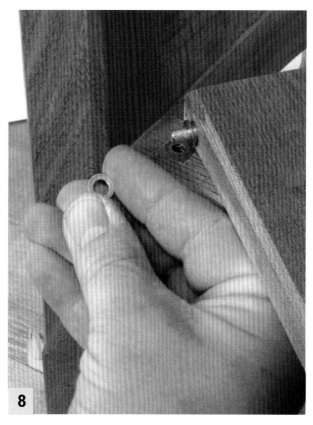

8

important that the screw shaft pivots in the stack of trapped washers, not in the wood, so the hinge will not wear and become sloppy. An extra washer between the doorframe and the rail defines the door's clearance.

Ball catches are let into holes drilled in the cabinet frame so they contact directly onto the wood of the doorframe, where shallow indents are drilled. This way, any marking of the wood by the ball will be on the rear underside of the door where it does not show.

THE TOP

If the top is to be used as a seat, the timber must be thick enough not to deflect, so I suggest using 1¼in (32mm) boards. The top is made from two half-width pieces butt-jointed together. To make the joint nearly invisible, clamp the two parts face to face in the vice, and shave the pair of edges together using a long plane. Having confirmed there is no gap, with the timber held edge to edge in front of a light, glue the panels in a butt joint. You need to consider safety when you design a

piece of furniture and if there are any potential hazards to the user, you need to protect against them. With the low height of this cupboard, I decided it was necessary to guard against someone banging their knees on the corner of the protruding lid. A curve on the edges guards against this and also makes the top more attractive. I suggest using a spokeshave for this task. A concave 550-type spokeshave will produce a smooth, rounded edge, but a flat-soled shave would also do the job with a little more patience.

The cabinet top is fixed at the back and sides by L-shaped buttons. The ends of these are dry-fitted into rebates, channelled near the upper edges of the side and back rails. The buttons are then screwed to the underside of the top. This technique will allow for seasonal movement of the top.

9 The top is shaped with a concave spokeshave.

10 L-shaped buttons slot into a rebate.

11 The buttons are screwed to the underside of the top.

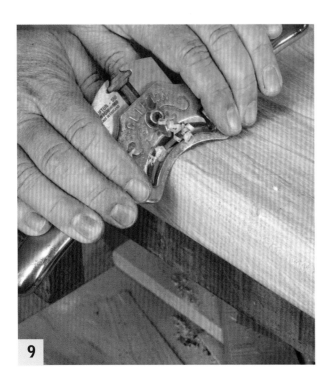

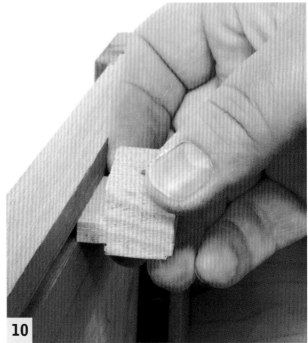

11

LININGS

The linings for this cabinet are the back panel
and the base panel. You may also want to fit a
shelf. Cedar of Lebanon is the traditional lining
timber for good-quality furniture because it is rot-
proof, it repels insects and it has an attractive scent
that stays fresh for years. Cedar is light in weight
and it cuts quite easily, but it is prone to large,
dead knots that, like those found in all softwoods,
need a very sharp-edged cutter to plane. The cedar
may need edge jointing to make large enough
panels. It can be butt-jointed or an intermediate
rail can be added with a rebate on each side to
join the half-width panels.

FINISHING

Danish oil looks beautiful on elm – it gives a good
depth of colour and preserves the real woody nature
of the finish, which has so many natural variations
in it. It needs to be thinned with white spirit, then
applied liberally with a brush, and allowed to soak
in for about 20 minutes. To produce a fine finish,
you must then rub the oil off with a cotton rag
before it dries, so there is no wetness left on the
surface. To build up the finish, give all the outside
faces three or four applications of Danish oil,
allowing a day's drying time between each. Brush
on then wipe off as before, sanding with a fine
paper between each coat. Finally, bring the finish
to a sheen with a beeswax paste.

Danish oil is not a durable finish so I suggest
you use a more hardwearing preparation on the
top for extra protection. To match the appearance
of Danish oil while also providing durability,
I recommend a high-quality yacht varnish, diluted
and applied in the same way. Build up a number
of thin layers, wiping each one off before it has
time to form a treacly coating. The resulting finish,
while slightly glossier than oil, is attractive and
impervious to liquids.

TO ROUT OR PLANE?

The rebating, fielding and edge-shaping
processes in this project could alternatively
have been performed with a router, fitted with
appropriate cutters. I use both methods,
depending on the job, weighing up the pros and
cons. For example, setting up a router takes
time and is noisy and dusty. If a mistake is
made the component can be ruined and the
surface left needs further finishing. On the other
hand, specialist planes can be expensive to buy
and do not cut as quickly as a router, but they
do leave a silky finish.

Oak bookcase

 Skill level 1 | Machinery used: router

This straightforward, almost minimal style of bookcase is designed to stand in a hall, a landing or a bedroom. Most of the work is performed with a router and just four cutters (see pages 92–99 for an introduction to routing).

ABOVE The finished bookcase.

Solid oak construction with chamfered edges, the wide top and the arched undersides are all features borrowed from early 1900s Arts and Crafts furniture. The arched undersides are quite functional – they ensure that, even on a thick carpet, all the weight is borne at the four corners, providing stability. The chamfered edges prevent splinters forming during the making and during the bookcase's use. The top shelf is divided into two square cubbyholes, the partition being helpful in keeping small books from falling over. Shelves below increase in size so that the size of each gap is 2in (50mm) taller than the one above it – this encourages heavy books to be placed at the bottom, again aiding stability.

All the shelves are fixed to the sides by sliding in dovetailed housing joints. Both sides are fixed to the top by the same method. In fact, these dovetailed housings are the only joints used, so once you have set up a system for routing joints like these repeatedly, the rest of the joint-cutting is like shelling peas. The back panel is let into a rebate, then screwed in place.

THE WOOD

Solid oak boards from a hardwood stockist are likely to originate from America, or possibly continental Europe. I used kiln-dried American 'white' oak for this project. It is available in large boards, clear of defects at a moderate price. It is prone to shakes. If these take the form of cracks near the end, be prepared to cut a few inches off before measuring out from the end of a board. Use marine ply for the rear panel with an outer veneer that matches the colour of the oak. The ply also helps to brace the structure and prevent strain on the housing joints.

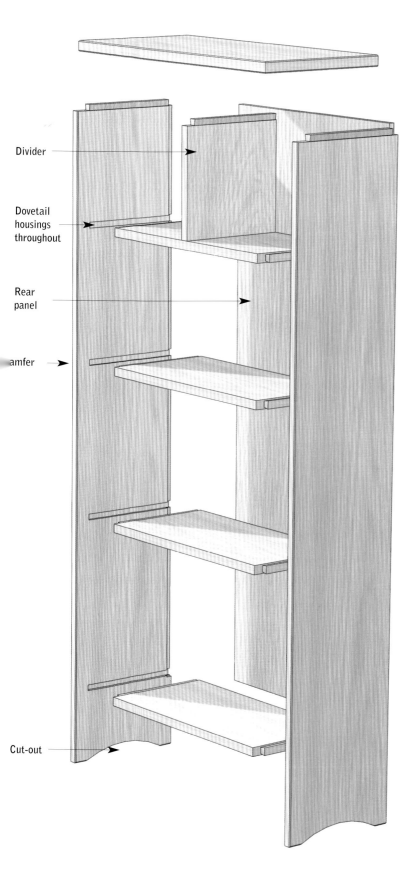

Divider

Dovetail
housings
throughout

Rear
panel

amfer

Cut-out

CONSTRUCTION

You could ask the wood yard that
supplies your timber to plane it
and cut it to size for the project.
The advantages of this approach
are that you can get straight on
with the construction work. There
are, however, a few things to watch
if you decide on this option. Firstly,
the crosscut facility in the yard may
not be straight and square, so
specify the timber over-length and
re-cut it straight in your workshop.
Secondly, if you are having the
wood planed, ensure that it has
been kept dry beforehand. For
indoor use, the moisture content
needs to be below 12%, as it will
normally be after kiln drying.

CUTTING LIST

- **2 x sides: oak**
  $9^3/_4$ x 53 x $^3/_4$in
  (250 x 1340 x 18mm)
- **1 x top shelf: oak**
  11 x 24 x $^7/_8$in
  (280 x 600 x 22mm)
- **4 x shelves: oak**
  9 x 18 x $^{23}/_{32}$in
  (225 x 460 x 18mm)
- **1 x top partition: oak**
  $8^3/_4$ x $9^1/_2$ x $^{23}/_{32}$in
  (220 x 240 x 18mm)
- **1 x rear panel: thick
  oak-faced ply**
  $18^3/_8$ x 48in x $^1/_2$in
  (470 x 1200 x 12mm)

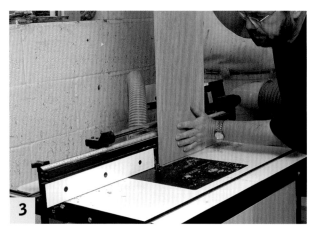

The problem is that, if the wood has been stored outside after kilning, it re-absorbs moisture. If it is planed in a damp condition then allowed to dry, it will almost certainly cup and possibly twist. Thirdly, the planer blades in a hardwood supplier will suffer a lot of hard work before sharpening. This means they may be blunt while your expensive timber passes through, with the result of torn grain. Be prepared to re-plane surfaces if this is the case and allow extra thickness accordingly.

1 Roughly measure out lengths from the oak boards.

2 After planing and thicknessing, cut to precise dimensions.

3 Sliding dovetails on the router table.

4 Dovetailed edgings are cut to fit into housings or dados.

DOVETAILED ENDS

The shelves are supported in housings cut into the sides, which are held between housings cut in the top panel. Dovetails in the housings mean these joints are locked in place with practically no possibility of working loose over the years.

If you use a router table, fit the dovetail bit and raise the height to ⁵⁄₁₆in (8mm), so this will be the depth of the dovetailed board ends. This will match the depth of the housings or dados. Adjust the fence so, at table level, the cutter will just clear the wood. That way the full width of the dovetail will be equal to the full thickness of the board.

If you wish to simplify the design, you could use plain, straight housing joints, with the advantage of being easier to fit. These would rely on the glue to keep them closed tightly, so they would still need to be carefully cut to ensure the glued surfaces met.

DOVETAILED HOUSINGS

Use a workshop-made router fence for housing joints – a large L-shaped piece of MDF. Carefully saw and plane this from ⅝in (15mm) thick sheet, then attach a strip of wood down one edge with screws and glue. To position the fence, first mark the required location of the cut. With the router turned off, lower the cutter to touch the wood and position the router so it is in the correct location. Gently slide the L-shaped fence up so it just touches the router base. Clamp the fence firmly in position using a pair of G-cramps or similar.

Cut the housings in two stages. For the first cut, use a straight-sided cutter bit. That way, you can plunge the depth of the housing in two or three progressively deeper passes and avoid forcing or burning the cutter. The second stage uses the dovetail bit to undercut the edges of the housing. You will need to make two passes, one for each side of the housing. Adjust the fence position between passes to ensure the correct width of housing matches the dovetailed ends on the boards.

Make sure the direction in which you move the router causes it to be pressed against the fence by the leading edge of the cutter. The dovetailed board ends and the housings finish slightly short of the front edges of the sides and shelves. I finished the joints about 1in (25mm) behind the front edge. When you fit the dovetails together it should be a snug fit. Try this by dry-fitting the joints, but not fully as they might jam causing damage.

5

6

7

8

9

5 Mark the distance between the housings beneath the top from the shoulders on a shelf. Allowance must be made for the shoulder width beneath the dovetail.

6 The L-shaped routing fence has a guide rail on the underside.

7 Position the router for the cut, then before clamping it, slide the fence against the router base.

8 Rout a housing or dado against the fence.

9 Dovetail the housing.

ARCHES FOR FEET

The lower ends of all of the boards that will form the sides have a segment cut out of them to leave an arch between a pair of feet. You can cut by the trammel arm method, rather like a compass. No special equipment is needed, just a router fitted with its sliding fence and a straight cutter bit.

If there is an existing hole in the far end of the sliding fence, use that. If not, drill one. This hole forms the pivot point with a round nail through it, hammered into a piece of scrap which is clamped to the bench top. Adjust the sliding fence arms so the router cutter swings around the nail in an arc with a radius of about 8in (200mm). Now clamp the side board in position under the router so it will leave a foot that is 1in (25mm) wide on each side of the board.

CHAMFERING

With the housing joints cut and tested, the edges of all the boards need chamfering before assembly. Make the chamfers narrow, a little less than ⁵⁄₆₄in (2mm). This is sufficient to remove any possibility of splintering. Use a 45° cutter fitted with a bearing guide. The cutting can be performed with the router handheld, in which case you need to clamp each piece, and re-clamp it to gain access to all the edges. I find this job easier and quicker on the router table. The chamfered edges left by a router cutter bit, especially if it is a TCT bit, can be a little furry. Use a small fine-set plane to finish them to a silky-smooth touch.

ASSEMBLY

Use a small glue brush to run PVA into each housing groove before finally sliding the dovetailed board ends into place. The wet PVA will act as a lubricant to help prevent jamming. A light tap with a soft-faced mallet may be required to drive the dovetailed housings together.

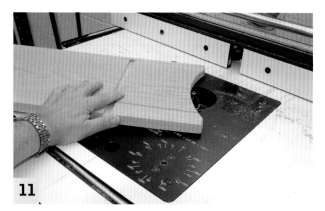

10 Cut arches to form the feet on the side panels.

11 Chamfer all the edges.

12 Be careful not to jam the joint when test-fitting the housings.

13 Test for square and wind while clamping up.

Apply sash cramps level with the shelves to pull them firmly together while the glue sets. While the glue is still soft, use an accurate try square to check the shelves and top are at right angles to the sides. Sight across the edge of one side to check the edge of other side is level with it and the carcass is not twisted or 'in wind'. If necessary, adjust the cramps to eliminate any distortion while the joints set.

BACK PANEL

The shelves are recessed at the front and rear by $\frac{1}{2}$in (13mm). The rear recess is to allow for the thickness of the plywood panel. In order to make space to screw the back panel onto the sides and the top, you need to cut rebates all around the inside edges of these parts. These rebates could be cut before the case is assembled, but they would have to be carefully stopped at each side of the top panel, part way through the dovetail housing joint. I chose instead to use a bearing-guided rebate cutter mounted in a handheld router after the glue had set and the clamps were removed.

The cutter leaves rounded corners in the rebates and it cannot cut past the shelves because they get in the way of the guide bearing. I used a wide-bladed chisel to square up the rebate after the router had done its job. The rear panel should be cut to size accurately with $\frac{1}{16}$in (1.5mm) clearance all around. Then drill and screw the panel into the rebate using 1in (25mm) No. 6 woodscrews every 3in (75mm) or so around the edge.

FINISHING

If you sand the individual components thoroughly before assembly, working through finer and finer grades, there will be very little preparation needed on the finished furniture. I decided to use Danish oil for this bookcase because it brings so much richness to oak compared to modern varnishes. Dilute the oil with white spirit and brush on generously. Wipe away the mixture after about 20 minutes, using a cotton cloth, before a skin forms.

This preserves the true surface nature of the wood. After applying several coats of oil, with one day's drying time between each, you can rub the surface over with beeswax paste polish and buff it with cotton to a sheen. Alternatively, leave the oil as a satin finish.

14 Rebates cut for the back panel.

15 Square out the rebate corners with a wide chisel.

16 Screw the back panel in place.

Oak bedside cabinets

  Skill level 2 | Machinery used: router

This pair of bedside cabinets introduce you to drawer-making (see also pages 62–67) and form the first part of a bedroom set that continues with a bed and wardrobe in the following projects.

ABOVE The finished cabinets.

I purchased wide boards of American oak for this project because, even though dealers charge more for these wider boards, they can be more efficient to use, as there is proportionately less wastage and sapwood. It may be possible to make the tops for these bedside cabinets from single, unjointed boards, as these can be very attractive when the end grain is visible. Otherwise, rip-saw the boards into suitable widths.

Prepare boards for butt jointing by planing the edges together as a pair. This causes any tilt of the plane from side to side on one edge, to be matched by an equal, but opposite, tilt on the corresponding edge, so they will butt together straight.

Before gluing, check that the board edges meet without gaps by placing one on top of another and sighting for any gap with a light behind. You can use butt joints with plain, glued edges for thick timber where there is plenty of long-grain contact area, but if you are not confident in a plain butt joint, use a biscuit jointer. It also helps with the alignment. The corner posts or legs are thicker American oak, normally sold as 2in (50mm) thick, rough-sawn stock. Rip-saw then plane and thickness it down to into 1⅝in (40mm) square sections for the corner posts or legs. All the material for the rails, tops and drawer sides is planed, thicknessed and dimensioned ready to start construction. The material for the slats must be re-sawn or thicknessed down to ⁹⁄₁₆in (15mm).

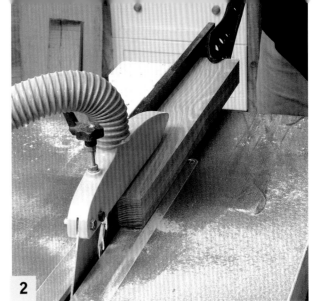

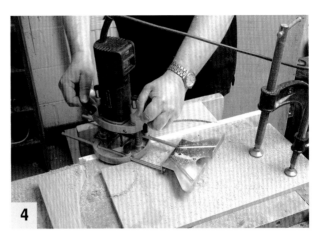

ARCHED RAILS

The arched undersides of the lower rails are a typical feature of this American-influenced Arts and Crafts style. I find the most successful and repeatable way to cut these is with a router on a trammel arm. Use the sliding fence that comes with the router – pivot it on a woodscrew fixed into an offcut, clamped to the bench. Arrange this so the cutter follows a suitable radius of arc on a piece of timber clamped in the bench vice. Clamp the oak behind a scrap piece of wood before routing the arc, otherwise the cutter will collide with the vice jaw or bench front. If the surface left by the router cutter is less smooth than normal, this is probably due to slack in the trammel arm or the pivot. The easiest solution then is to finish the inside of the arc with a compass plane or a spokeshave.

The cabinet requires four lower rails and three upper ones; there is no rail at the top front because the full-height drawer occupies this position. The posts are 1½in (40mm) thick so they are ample to take two mortices at right angles to each other at the same height, without any issues over placing the joints. I centred all mortices in the posts and centred all the tenons on the rails. Cutting mortices

1 Both cabinet tops are glued and butt-jointed.

2 Thick stock is ripped into square sections for the legs.

3 The material for the legs, rails, tops and drawers is planed, thicknessed and dimensioned ready to start construction.

4 The arched undersides of the lower rails are cut with a router on a trammel arm.

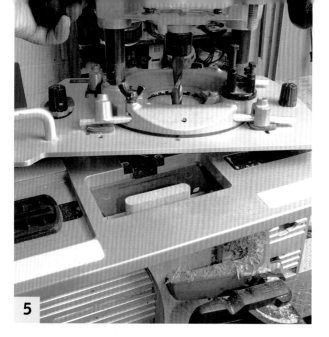

5

6

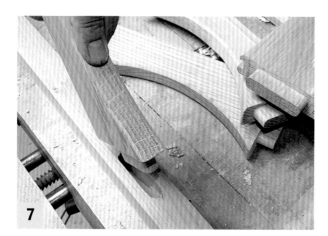

7

with a router and guide fence is straightforward, but making the round-ended tenons to fit can be trickier. However, frame mortice and tenon jigs are extremely versatile and make easy work of simple joints like these. The main advantage is that it is simple to centre the joint and, once the jig has been initially set up, the joints fit every time. I always partly dry fit joints to test them before gluing but with a jig like this, it is unnecessary.

SLATS

In this project I show a different technique for fixing slats than the one used for the matching bed (see page 145). However, either technique can be used. The vertical slats in each side frame are made from stock, planed down to ⁹⁄₁₆in (15mm) thick. Accurate cutting is crucial for these slats. The slats in each set must all be identical in length to avoid producing gaps in the joints with the lower and upper rails. An end stop on the table saw fence is the best way to achieve this.

Cut stub-tenons on the vertical slats to allow them to be fixed in slots, routed in the rails. This allows the slats to be slid into place and eliminates the problem that I experienced in assembling the dowelled slats of the matching bed. The tenons can be quite short and the slot shallow because there is no structural force on these parts. They effectively do the same job as side panels would, and panels are normally loosely fitted in a slot.

5 Cutting tenons on the rails using a frame mortice and tenon jig.

6 Mortices in the legs are cut with the jig.

7 Test-fitting the mortice and tenon joints.

8 Stub-mortices on the vertical slats slide into the slotted rails.

8

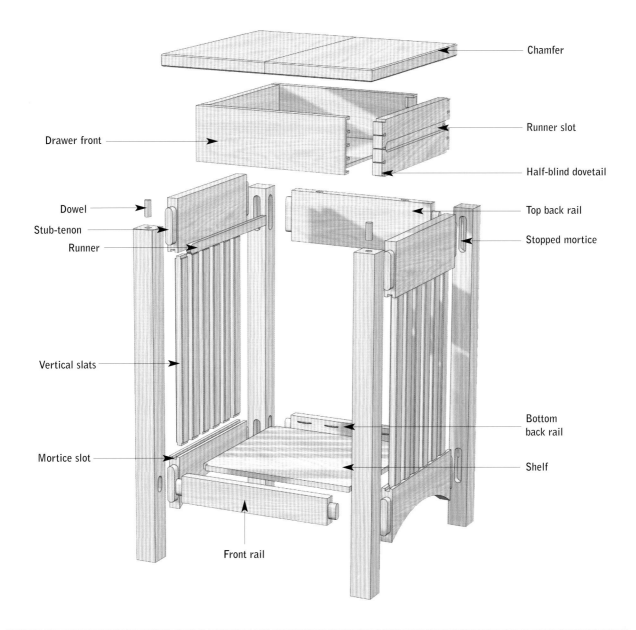

Chamfer

Runner slot

Drawer front

Half-blind dovetail

Dowel

Stub-tenon

Runner

Top back rail

Stopped mortice

Vertical slats

Bottom back rail

Mortice slot

Shelf

Front rail

CUTTING LIST

- **8 x corner posts: oak**
  $1^5/_8$ x $1^5/_8$ x $24^3/_8$in (40 x 40 x 620mm)
- **24 x side slats: oak**
  $^9/_{16}$ x 1 x $14^3/_{16}$in (15 x 25 x 360mm)
- **4 x lower side rails: oak**
  $^7/_8$ x 4 x $12^3/_{16}$in (22 x 100 x 310mm)
- **4 x upper side rails: oak**
  $^7/_8$ x 4 x $12^3/_{16}$in (22 x 100 x 310mm)
- **2 x lower back rails: oak**
  $^{23}/_{32}$ x 2 x $14^3/_{16}$in (18 x 50 x 360mm)
- **2 x lower front rails: oak**
  $^{23}/_{32}$ x 2 x $14^3/_{16}$in (18 x 50 x 360mm)
- **2 x upper back rails: oak**
  $^{23}/_{32}$ x 4 x $14^3/_{16}$in (18 x 100 x 360mm)

- **2 x drawer backs: oak**
  $^{23}/_{32}$ x 4 x $12^3/_{16}$in (18 x 100 x 310mm)
- **2 x drawer fronts: oak**
  $^{23}/_{32}$ x 4 x $12^3/_{16}$in (18 x 100 x 310mm)
- **4 x drawer sides: oak**
  $^{23}/_{32}$ x 4 x $12^3/_{16}$in (18 x 100 x 310mm)
- **4 x drawer runners: oak**
  $^{23}/_{32}$ x $^{23}/_{32}$ x $9^3/_4$in (18 x 18 x 250mm)
- **2 x lower shelf panels: oak**
  $^3/_8$ x $11^3/_8$ x $13^3/_8$in (10 x 290 x 340mm)
- **2 x top panels: oak**
  $^7/_8$ x $14^3/_{16}$ x $16^9/_{16}$in (22 x 360 x 420mm)
- **2 x drawer bottoms: ply**
  $^1/_4$ x $11^3/_8$ x $11^3/_8$in (6 x 290 x 290mm)

OAK BEDSIDE CABINETS **139**

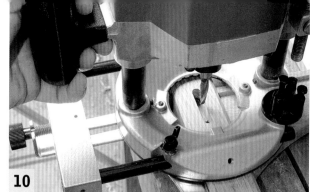

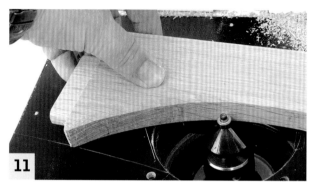

The easiest way to cut these is to machine them on the router table, using a sliding fence. If your table is not fitted with a sliding fence, you can improvise one by sliding a thick, square MDF block against the rear fence. To keep the slats at the required spacing and hide the slots in the rails where they are exposed in the gaps between slats, I cut infill blocks on the bandsaw and press into place between the rails.

9 Infill blocks separate the slats, hiding the slots in the rails.

10 Routing of mortice slots for the front and rear rails in the posts.

11 Components are chamfered on the router table before assembly.

12 The lower shelf, made from thinner solid oak, is biscuit-jointed.

CHAMFERS

I like to shave chamfered edges around all components so there is no risk of splinters. This is typical of Arts and Crafts furniture, but is also a very practical one, which can be used on all styles. It is more effective to chamfer edges on parts before you assemble them. With a stack prepared and ready for assembly it is quite easy to run them across the router table, fitted with a bearing-guided bevel-trim cutter. Sanding is also often easier at this stage than when the parts are assembled. The lower shelf is effectively a panel trapped in slots routed in the four lower rails. Make this from oak re-sawn down to ⅜in (10mm) thick. This will need to be either biscuit-jointed or joined with a loose tongue.

DRAWERS

Drawers are best made with dovetail joints (see page 62–67). The convention is to use lapped dovetails at the front so they do not show and through dovetails at the back, which are normally made from thinner wood to match the sides. This is because conventional drawers slide between top and bottom rails known as 'kickers' and 'runners' in a framework, so they have sides and backs made from thin material to keep their weight down.

The drawers for this cabinet, however, are side-hung on rails fixed inside the cabinet. These rails run in broad slots, routed into the sides of the drawers. This means using thicker material so the guide slots can be deep enough to avoid undue wear.

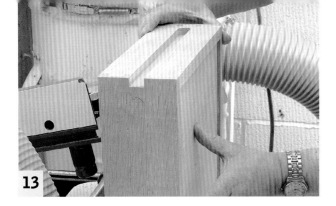

13 Slots are routed in the drawer sides to accept the fixed rails.

14 Dovetail joints for the drawers are routed with a jig.

15 PVA glue is brushed into the dovetail sockets.

16 Individual parts are easier to access for sanding.

Use uniform-thickness oak for all four sides of the drawers, cutting the same lapped dovetails for the front and rear joints. Having set the jig up and tested it on a scrap sample, you can quickly run off a set of eight identical dovetail joints for the two drawers. The guide rails are $\frac{1}{16}$in (1.5mm) narrower than the slots that they run in. They are also waxed so they do not bind. After trial-fitting in the drawer sides, the guide rails should be screwed in place inside of the upper cabinet rails.

TOP FITTING

The top needs to able to expand and contract across the grain with changes in humidity, without applying stress to the frame or splitting itself. This is achieved by screwing the top to the back rail through slotted holes, permitting the back edge of

the top to move backwards and forwards. The front edge of the top is fixed to the front corner posts with $\frac{1}{2}$in (13mm) diameter dowels. With grain running side to side, the top fixes the gap between the posts for the drawers to slide between, acting as a top rail for the framework. Drill the posts first, then fit dowel pins in the holes and lower the top into its correct position. Apply pressure to the top so the pins mark drilling positions on its underside.

FINISHING

Sand all the bedside cabinet parts before assembly. For the final finish, apply a coat of Danish oil and white spirit mixture, soak it into the wood then wipe off before it sets. Leave to dry for two days, then sand all accessible areas with a random-orbit machine. Repeat with another coat and wipe off half an hour later. Mix in some yacht varnish to make the top surface more durable. Leave to dry for a week, then apply beeswax paste to help keep the cabinets clean and pleasing to touch. Apply beeswax or wax paste to the bare wood on the drawer sides and runners, to give a smooth action.

Oak bed

  Skill level 2 | Machinery used: router, bandsaw

This Arts and Crafts-inspired bed matches the bedside cabinets in the previous project and also makes use of some routing skills (see page 92–99 for more details about routing).

Based on the Arts and Crafts style, this wide double bed with its 64 vertical slats would be a daunting project if they all had to be planed and jointed by hand. The generously proportioned bedstead will carry a conventional modern divan base for extra comfort and provide a good height.

TIMBER PREPARATION

Most of the oak for the bed was cut from 1in (25mm) rough-sawn oak boards, while I used 2½in (60mm) rough-sawn material for the posts and 1⅛in (28mm) for the side rails. I bought all the oak and stored it in my warm, dry workshop

BELOW Finished bed in the workshop.

for a month before using my own machines to mill it to the cutting list. Alternatively, you could hand over the cutting list to a good hardwood supplier and ask them to prepare the parts for you. Make sure that the timber is thoroughly dry and has been kept dry before it is machined. A common problem occurs when timber, which has been kiln dried, is stored in less-than-ideal conditions. The wood fibres, with around 10% moisture content, are thirsty to soak up water from wherever they can find it, and outdoor air or a damp workshop provides plenty. The result is an uneven moisture content, so after the wood is machined, it continues drying at different rates, twisting and cupping in the process.

SHAPING ARCHES

The arches on the underside of the lower rails are an important feature of the Arts and Crafts styling and they are quite straightforward to produce with any router. First, you must clamp the rail firmly to a bench, with the clamps well clear of the underside to allow the router to pass. You will also need a long trammel arm. This is simply a wooden baton made from scrap and screwed to the router base. It does, however, take a fair bit of space to operate. It may be necessary to rearrange the workshop temporarily or open the doors to accommodate the trammel and router arrangement.

1 A trammel arm shapes the arched underside of the lower rails.

2 After planing and thicknessing, mortices are routed in the corner posts.

The far end of the baton needs a hole drilled as a snug fit around the plain shaft of a woodscrew. Drive the screw into a scrap of softwood and clamp onto a surface at the same height as the bench. Now the router will work as a giant compass, pivoting around the screw shaft with a radius equal to the length of the arm. I found the ideal length to be 10ft (3m), for producing an arc about 3in (75mm) deep in rail. This removes half the thickness from the rail, leaving 3in (75mm) behind – quite adequate in view of the fact this rail does not support any weight. Have a dummy run at it with the router turned off and the cutter flush, to make sure it follows the required track for a symmetrically curved cutaway, before taking the plunge.

MORTICE AND TENONS

All mortice and tenon joints should be as strong as possible. This is particularly important on a bed that has to carry the weight of two people. Large double mortice and tenon joints carry the side rails but these come later, once the head- and tailboard are assembled.

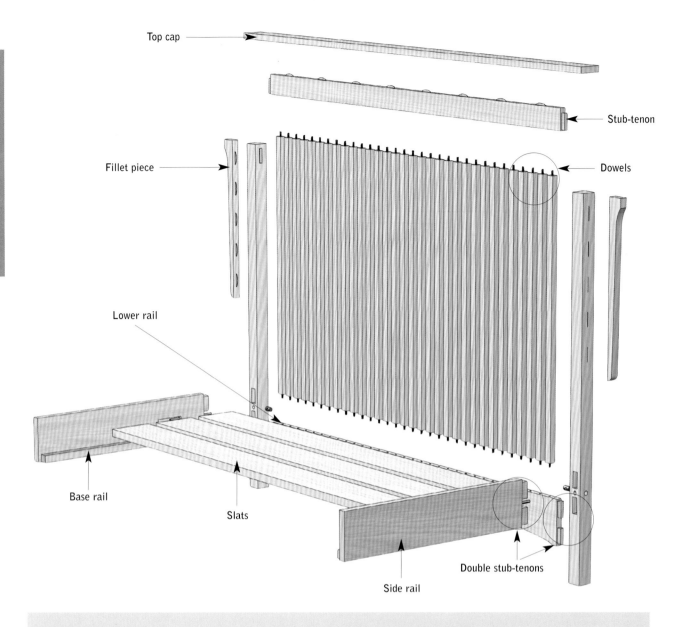

Top cap

Stub-tenon

Fillet piece

Dowels

Lower rail

Base rail

Slats

Side rail

Double stub-tenons

CUTTING LIST

- **2 x head posts: oak**
  47 x 2 x 2in (1200 x 50 x 50mm)
- **2 x foot posts: oak**
  35½ x 2 x 2in (900 x 50 x 50mm)
- **32 x head slats: oak**
  35½ x 1 x $^{25}/_{32}$in (900 x 25 x 20mm)
- **32 x foot slats: oak**
  23½ x 1 x $^{25}/_{32}$in (600 x 25 x 20mm)
- **2 x lower rails: oak**
  62 x 6 x $^{25}/_{32}$in (1580 x 150 x 20mm)
- **2 x upper rails: oak**
  62 x 2¾ x $^{25}/_{32}$in (1580 x 70 x 20mm)
- **2 x top caps: oak**
  70 x 3 x $^{25}/_{32}$in (1780 x 75 x 20mm)

- **2 x fillet pieces: oak**
  22 x 2 x 1in (560 x 50 x 25mm)
- **2 x side rails: oak**
  81 x 6 x 1in (2060 x 150 x 25mm)
- **2 x base rails: oak**
  78 x 1 x 1in (2000 x 25 x 25mm)
- **11 x base slats: pine**
  61 x 6 x 1in (1550 x 150 x 25mm)
- **2 x webbing: canvas**
  78 x 2in (2000 x 50mm)
- **4 x M6 steel bolts**
- **4 x M6 steel washers**
- **4 x M6 steel dowel nuts**

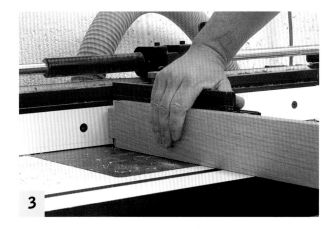

3

SLATS

The vertical rails or slats in the head and footboards are made from stock planed down to $^{25}/_{32}$in (20mm) thick. Accurate cutting is crucial for these slats. Each set must be identical in length to avoid producing gaping joints with the lower and upper rails. An end stop on the saw is the best way to achieve this. With the ends cut true and square, a dowel hole should be drilled in each centre. I used a lip and spur bit mounted in a drill in a rigid stand, temporarily mounted over the bench vice.

A scrap block clamped in the vice provides a locating guide to ensure the holes are central in each end of every slat. You could use either $^{5}/_{16}$in (8mm) or $^{3}/_{8}$in (10mm) dowels, and of course, a drill size to match. Ready-cut beech-wood dowels are better than cutting lengths off a smooth round rod, because they are fluted to allow glue to flow around them. Ensure the holes are deep enough –

The corner posts also have mortices in each side for conventional single mortice and tenon joints at low level for the lower rail and at the top for the upper rail. These joints will be glued and they do not carry a significant load, so $^{1}/_{2}$in (13mm) width joints should be fine. I cut the tenon cheeks on the router table using a sliding fence to guide the rail across the cutter. The mortices can be cut with a plunge action, using the sliding fence against the vice jaws to guide the router. Once the mortices have been cut to full depth, the ends are squared up using a mortice chisel and mallet. Dry-fit the joints, but do not glue them yet as the slats need to be trapped between upper and lower rails first.

3 Tenons are cut on the router table.

4 Vertical slats are cut in two lengths for the head and foot ends.

5 A temporary jig is set up around the vice for repeatable dowel holes in the slats.

4

5

OAK BED   **145**

6

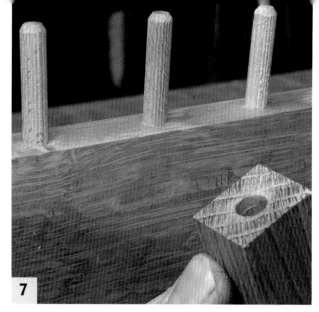

7

each one should be just over half the length of the dowel – otherwise the dowel might prevent the joint closing.

The same drill and vice arrangement can be used to prepare holes in the upper and lower rails, but first the positions need to be accurately marked at regular intervals for even spacing. Avoid using repetitive measurements of the gaps between hole centres as the errors will build up. Instead, take a calculator and work out the spacing by dividing the distance between tenon shoulders by the number of slats plus one – that is 33 in the case of this bed. Now add this spacing repeatedly as you mark the position of each centre hole on the rail. Having marked out one rail, the positions of the dowel holes can be transferred to the other three using a try square. Ensure there is enough glue in each socket to slide up around the dowel, but not enough to squeeze out from the joint – I use a nozzled bottle to insert the glue then a brush to spread it around the sides.

Aligning all the dowels as you press the rails together takes patience. Start at one end and work your way progressively along. With all 64 dowels inserted, use sash cramps to pull the upper and lower rails together. The waste piece cut from under the arch on the lower rail can be temporarily replaced to provide a flat surface for the clamp jaws.

HEADBOARD AND FOOT

With the rails and slats dowelled and glued, the corner post mortices are ready for gluing. If these were previously dry-fitted, it should be possible to glue and clamp them together without applying any significant strain to the dowel joints on the slats. The distance between posts will be around 63in (1600mm) so you need either to use long sash cramps or, as I did, use canvass or nylon band cramps.

8

6 The dowelling arrangement is used on the upper and lower rails.

7 Dowels are inserted in the rails ready for the first stage of glue-up.

8 Rails and slats dowelled and glued with corner post mortices are ready for gluing.

BOLTED MORTICE AND TENONS

With the headboard and footboard glued up and assembled, it is time to turn your attention to the side rails, which hold them together and carry the weight of the bed onto the corner posts. The joints are large double tenons, pulled together with 4in (100mm) long M6 steel bolts. Dowel nuts fit between the double mortices through holes in the side of each post. Their holes are then plugged.

I chose to use full 1in (25mm) thick boards for the rails, which were 6in (150mm) wide. As well as preventing them from flexing, this also allows the joints to be made large and rigid. Use a $^{25}/_{32}$in (20mm) straight cutter to plunge each pair of mortices, again squaring up the ends with a mortice chisel and mallet. The tenons can again be cut on the router table, although the cut is shallow because the shoulders are narrow. Remove the centre part between each pair of tenons with a fine router bit, using pieces of scrap clamped in place as a guide.

9 A fine router is used to cut the shoulder between a double tenon.

10 The remaining shoulders are shaped on the router table.

11 Double mortices are cut in the corner posts.

12 A slot is routed to accept the bolts securing the mortice and tenon joints between side rails and corner posts.

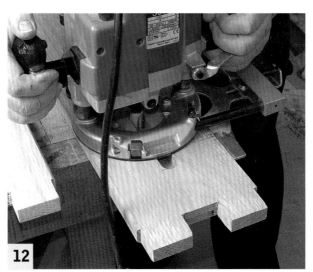

against, so square it up with a mortice chisel and mallet. It is necessary to drill an accurately aligned hole in the gap between the double tenons for the bolt shaft to pass through. With the side rails, being 81in (2060mm) long, there was no possibility of positioning them under a vertical drill press so I used the lathe as a horizontal boring machine. Cutting the large double mortice and tenon joints and aligning the bolt holes requires a good deal of care. The finished joints must pull up tight for strength; the load is borne by the wooden mortice and tenons while the steel bolts are there to prevent them working apart.

BISCUITING

With the head- and footboards constructed and temporarily bolted together in the workshop, the top caps and decorative fillets under the corners need to be fitted. The fillets need shaping, for which I used French curves to mark out a template, followed by the bandsaw for cutting. A spokeshave can then be used to fair the curve and chamfer the outer edges. These parts are not load bearing, so you can use the biscuit jointer to fix them in place. However, having said that, there is always the risk that someone will incorrectly try to move the bed by pressing on or lifting under the top caps, so use plenty of biscuits together with an even spread of glue.

DIVAN SUPPORTS

The purpose of this bedstead is to be able to support a modern divan base, nominally 5ft wide by 6ft, 6in long (1524 x 1981mm). Bed-makers work to loose dimensions, so allow an extra 1in (25mm) each way, but also fit slats under the base in case it is undersized. The slats are made from 1in (25mm) thick pine and rested on square oak rails, glued and screwed to the lower inside edge of each side rail. The slats rest in place but to prevent them moving, staple lengths of upholsterers webbing between them and fit dowels to locate the end slats.

To allow the bolt to be fitted, mill a 4in (100mm) long slot using the $^{25}/_{32}$in (20mm) cutter. The position of this slot must allow the bolt to tighten in the dowel nut. The outside end of the slot needs to be flat for the bolt head and washer to press

13 The lathe is used as a horizontal borer for a bolt hole between the tenons.

14 M6 bolts and washers are trial-fitted in the side rails.

15 M6 dowel nuts are fitted in the corner posts between double mortices.

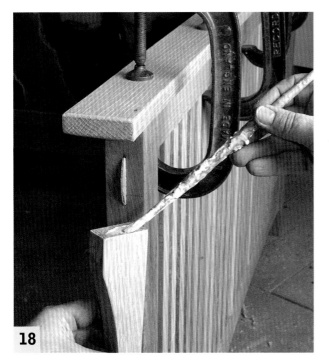

If you were going to build a bed like this to be able to support a mattress directly, rather than with a divan, I would suggest supporting the slats towards the top of the side rails with edgewise reinforcing pieces beneath to form a T-shape and stop them from sagging.

FINISHING

Although the bed is simple in principle, it contains many parts that will need sanding and finishing. I recommend you do most of the preparation before the bed is assembled, that way you can sand into the corners unobstructed. For the final finish, use three coats of Danish oil, soaked into the wood then wipe off before it sets and repeat the process at intervals of one day.

16 The top caps are biscuit-jointed to the rails.

17 Fillet pieces are roughly shaped with the bandsaw then faired with a spokeshave.

18 Fillet pieces are biscuit-jointed and glued in place.

19 Arts and Crafts feature chamfers are cut on all the outer edges.

20 Webbing is stapled between softwood slats to hold them in place while the bed base is lowered into place.

Oak wardrobe

  Skill level 2 | Machinery used: router, planers and thicknessers, table saw, bandsaw

Arts and Crafts in style, this wardrobe is a timeless design made to complete the bedroom suite along with the king-sized bed (page 142) and the bedside cabinets (page 136).

ABOVE The finished wardrobe.

The two drawers of this wardrobe are graded in size, the lower one being slightly deeper, as are the horizontal rails of the doorframes. These effects collaborate with the subtle taper of the 6ft 6in (2m) corner posts to keep this massive cabinet looking slender and elegant while its feet are firmly planted on the floor. The doors are made with book-matched panels of solid oak so that the pattern in each one is a mirror image of the other. The exterior is made from solid American white oak, except for the back panel against the wall and the central panel of the top which are both marine ply. The drawer fronts and sides are solid oak with lapped dovetail joints, while the drawer backs and bottoms are also marine ply.

POST AND RAIL

The wardrobe consists of a low drawer unit, which acts as a base for the upper carcass. This is made from separate panelled sub-assemblies, allowing the large piece to be easily transported and dismantled if it is necessary. The entire framework is mortice and tenon jointed. Dry-fitted dowel pegs are used to keep the upper and lower sections of the corner posts in good alignment. The rails at the base of the side panels are fixed to the rails at the top of the chest of drawers using screwed blocks of oak. The rear panel is fixed to the top of the chest of drawers and the side panels by the same method. The back braces the upper structure, preventing any twisting.

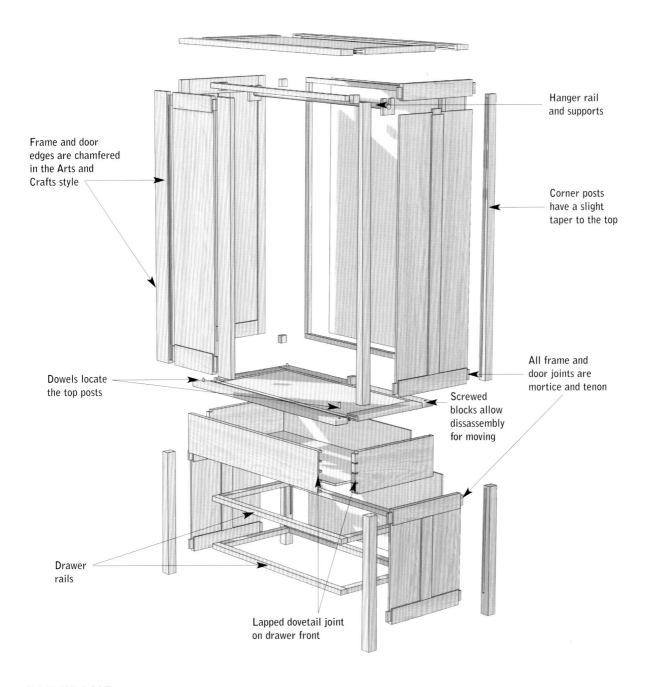

Hanger rail and supports

Frame and door edges are chamfered in the Arts and Crafts style

Corner posts have a slight taper to the top

Dowels locate the top posts

All frame and door joints are mortice and tenon

Screwed blocks allow dissassembly for moving

Drawer rails

Lapped dovetail joint on drawer front

OAK FRAME

The four corner posts for this wardrobe are taper rip-sawn from a 2in (50mm) thick board. The posts are cut to the full 6ft 6in (2m) length on the table saw and then planed to 1in (25mm) at the top and 2in (50mm) at the bottom. This means that the corner posts have a square footprint, but a narrow rectangular top to match the top rail. Each post is cross-sawn into two pieces, $25\frac{1}{2}$in (650mm) long at the broad end to form the corner post of the drawer unit and $53\frac{1}{2}$in (1350mm) long at the

narrow end to form the vertical rails or stiles of the side sub-assemblies. A simple way to cut mortice slots without jigs is to clamp the posts in a bench vice, with a tapered softwood wedge between the jaws and the tapered surface of the posts. A straight piece of hardwood clamped to the bench top and parallel to the vice functions as a fence to slide the router base against. Having cut rails to length for the drawer carcass and the upper carcass from 1in (25mm) thick boards, cut tenons on them. One

CUTTING LIST

4 x corner posts: oak
79 x 2 x 2in tapering to 1in (2000 x 50 x 50mm) tapering to 25mm). Each post is cross-sawn into a 25½in (650mm) length for the drawer unit and a 53½in (1350mm) length for one of the side sub-assemblies

DRAWER UNIT
2 x top rails: oak
3 x 1 x 43½in (75 x 25 x 1100mm)
2 x top side rails: oak
3 x 1 x 19¾in (75 x 25 x 500mm)
1 x panel: ply
18¾ x 39½ x ⅜in (475 x 1000 x 10mm)
1 x lower rail: oak
5 x 1 x 41½in (125 x 25 x 1050mm)
4 x drawer rails: oak
1½ x 1 x 41½in (40 x 25 x 1050mm)
4 x drawer runners: oak
1½ x 1 x 19¾in (40 x 25 x 500mm)
1 x drawer front: oak
8 x 1 x 39½in (200 x 25 x 1000mm)
2 x drawer sides: oak
8 x 1 x 18¾in (200 x 25 x 475mm)
1 x drawer back: ply
8 x ⅜ x 38½in (200 x 10 x 980mm)
1 x drawer front: oak
9 x 1 x 39½in (225 x 25 x 1000mm)
2 x drawer sides: oak
9 x 1 x 18½in (225 x 25 x 475mm)
1 x drawer back: ply
9 x ⅜ x 38½in (225 x 10 x 980mm)
2 x drawer bases: ply
17¾ x 38½ x ⅜in (450 x 980 x 10mm)
4 x side rails: oak
19¾ x 3 x 1in (500 x 75 x 25mm)
2 x side muntins: oak
19¾ x 3 x 1in (500 x 75 x 25mm)

4 x side panels: oak
19¾ x 8½ x ⅜in (500 x 220 x 10mm)

TWO SIDE SUB-ASSEMBLIES
4 x side rails: oak
19¾ x 3 x 1in (500 x 75 x 25mm)
2 x side muntins: oak
49 x 3 x 1in (1250 x 75 x 25mm)
4 x side panels: oak
49 x 8½ x ⅜in (1250 x 220 x 10mm)

TWO DOORS
2 x top rails: oak
15¾ x 3 x 1in (400 x 75 x 25mm)
2 x lower rails: oak
15¾ x 4 x 1in (400 x 100 x 25mm)
4 x vertical stiles: oak
52½ x 4 x 1in (1325 x 100 x 25mm)
2 x panels: oak
46½ x 12½ x ⅜in (1180 x 325 x 10mm)

TOP SUB-ASSEMBLY
2 x top rails: oak
3 x 1 x 45½in (75 x 25 x 1150mm)
2 x top side rails: oak
3 x 1 x 21½in (75 x 25 x 550mm)
1 x panel: ply
19¾ x 47½ x ⅜in (500 x 1100 x 10mm)
1 x over-door rail: oak
1 x 1 x 39½in (25 x 25 x 1000mm)

BACK SUB-ASSEMBLY
1 x panel: ply
39½ x 53½ x ⅜in (1000 x 1350 x 10mm)
2 x top and bottom battens: oak
39½ x 1 x 1in (1000 x 25 x 25mm)
2 x side battens: oak
53½ x 1 x 1in (1350 x 25 x 25mm)

method is using the router table with a large diameter straight cutter and a sliding fence. Panels for the doors and side sub-assemblies need to be made from thinner solid oak than the frame – otherwise the wardrobe would be excessively heavy and cumbersome as well as consuming vast amounts of material. Ideally, you need ½in (13mm) or thinner material, but you are unlikely to find this in a wood yard. Of course, if you wanted to you could reduce 1in (25mm) material by passing

it through a thicknesser but this would be very wasteful and would deny you the opportunity to make book-matched panels. A solution is to re-saw the oak by passing it on edge through a bandsaw.

The bandsaw must have a large depth capacity and a high-sided fence parallel to the blade. Even so, it would be very difficult to saw the full width of the panels in one go. Instead, I recommend ripping the boards into a number of narrower sections before re-sawing them on the bandsaw.

PANEL JOINTS

If you want the panel joints to be near invisible, the edges must be planed to fit together accurately. The way to achieve this is to clamp them face-to-face before planing the mating edges together as a pair using a long plane such as a No. 7 'jointer'. When the edges of the two panels are true, pairs of full-length shavings emerge from the plane mouth. Because the boards are thin, it may be difficult to glue them edge-to-edge in a butt joint without a

1 Full-height corner posts taper-cut on the table saw.

2 Mortice slots routed in the bench vice.

3 Tenons are shaped on the router table using a sliding fence.

4 Joints are tested by dry fitting while slots between the mortices will house panels.

5 When the edges are true, pairs of full-length shavings emerge from the No. 7 plane.

6 Biscuit jointing helps keep the panel edges aligned.

7 Before the panels are fitted the dry-jointed frames are chamfered internally.

8 Drawer sides and fronts are lap dovetailed.

9 The shoulders of the dovetails are trimmed with a backsaw.

10 The joints are fitted around the plywood drawer base.

little help. Use the biscuit jointer and insert a series of compressed beech-wood biscuits to keep the panel edges aligned while the glue is setting.

CHAMFERS

Chamfer edges on components before you assemble them. With a stack of parts prepared and ready for assembly it is then quite easy to run them across the router table, fitted with a bearing-guided bevel-trim cutter. Before fitting the door and side panels, dry-fit the frames and chamfer around the insides of them. This causes the chamfer to run neatly up to a stop at the corner joint in the frame. Sanding is also easier at this stage. Panels trapped in frames are near impossible to sand right to the edges when assembled. The payback for this preparation is that once the furniture is assembled there is less work involved in finishing it.

DRAWERS

Drawers need to have well-fitted dovetail joints between front and sides. The convention is to use lapped dovetails at the front so they do not show and through dovetails at the back, which are normally made from thinner wood to match the sides. Because the drawers were so large, I wanted to keep the weight down so I used ⅜in (8mm) thick marine plywood for the back and base. The back panel and base were both fitted in slots routed in the sides of the drawer.

Cut the dovetails using a router-based dovetailing jig. The drawers slide between top and bottom rails in the framework known as kickers and runners. These are often dry-fitted with a mortice and tenon into front and rear rails between the corner posts so they do not force the carcass apart by resisting wood movement in the sides. However, the sides of this carcass have horizontal rails so they will not conflict with the runners and kickers. This means that all the components can be glued in place, making a more rigid framework.

The drawers are fitted into the chest after planing the edges for a snug fit. A rub of wax on every sliding surface will turn this into a gliding action.

DOORS

Having previously made up the wide, thin door panels, you can clamp the frame parts around them. Check that the figuring is right before cutting them to length, mortice and tenoning and routing an inner groove to receive the panel edges.

Use band-cramps for gluing up the doors and side frames. To hold the doors shut, I fitted bullet-style ball-catches in the frame. These spring into the hollows that I scooped out with a gouge on the underside of each door.

The back panel was made from a single sheet of marine ply with 1in (25mm) square oak screwed and glued around all four edges. This panel has an important function, other than stopping the wardrobe contents falling out the back – it braces the upper structure and prevents racking. The side sub-assemblies are similarly fitted with screwed and glued blocks along the top and bottom edges, allowing them to be assembled after delivery using screws without glue into the drawer unit below and the top sub-assembly. To support coat hangers in the upper cabinet I fitted a single oak rail, which rests in a pair of slotted oak support brackets, one on each vertical intermediate side rail or muntin.

11 Truing drawer fronts to a snug fit in the carcass – be ambidextrous and use the plane either way!

12 Doorframes and panels are clamped in position to check the figuring is harmonious.

13 Bullet-style ball-catch in the frame springs into a hollow detent under the door.

14 A coat hanger rail sits in slotted oak supports.

FINISHING

If you have sanded all the parts before assembly, only a minimal amount of sanding will be necessary on the finished cabinets. For the final finish, apply a coat of Danish oil and white spirit mixture; soak it into the wood then wipe it off before it sets. Leave to dry for two days, and then sand all accessible areas with a random-orbit machine. Repeat with another coat, wiped off half an hour later. Apply beeswax or wax paste to the bare wood on the drawer sides and runners to give the drawers a smooth action. I fitted bronzed metal handles with back plates onto the drawers. These have concave edges, echoing the arch of the wardrobe's lower rail, and they are embossed with an attractive foursquare motif.

Coopered box

   Skill level 3 | Machinery used: router, bandsaw

Dovetailing, and frame and panelling are two methods of dealing with seasonal movement in solid-wood furniture. This elaborate coopered panel box combines these techniques in a dovetailed frame.

ABOVE Dry fitting the dovetails.

Coopering is the name given to forming a curved wooden component by butt jointing a series of strips with angled edges, rather like the staves of a barrel. We will also look at a method of cutting fine dovetails using the bandsaw in a system based on the handsaw technique. The technique is still reliant on hand and eye skills, but this time the machine accelerates the pace. For grooving, I used the router rather than a plough plane, for its ability to make curved slots with stopped ends. Fitting the router under a router-table enables you to use it like a miniature spindle-moulder, providing better control for jobs like rebating edges.

SHOOTING BOARD

The shooting board is a simple jig that helps you hand plane accurate right angles on the edge or end grain of a component. It consists of an accurately prepared solid board with a wide, shallow groove along one edge in which a plane will lay on its side. The groove is wide enough to take the full depth of the plane's side for maximum stability, and it is just deep enough so the edge of the mouth and the cutter are above it. The groove base must be flat and parallel to the board's surface to ensure the cutter is at right angles. An end stop, screwed onto the board perpendicular to the groove, locates the wood while you hold it down with hand pressure and plane its edges.

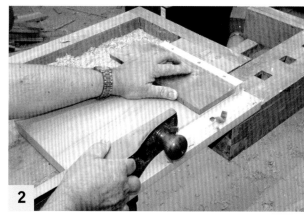

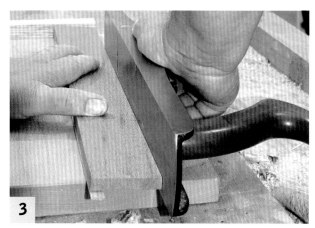

COOPERING

The idea of coopering is to build a close approximation to an arch, as a succession of flat sections that can later be blended into a continuous curve by planing the surfaces. I used ³⁄₈in (10mm) thick boards to avoid too much weight in the coopered lid, and to allow it to flex a little. Start with a wide panel, or more than one if necessary to cover the width, and slice it up into strips

1 Wide, thin boards ready for sawing into strips and coopering.

2 The shooting board is a jig for planing edges.

3 With a shim under the far side, the shooting board helps you plane an angled edge.

4 The boards are butt jointed and pulled with a band-cramp to form an approximate curve.

approximately 1½in (38mm) wide. Before cutting, pencil-mark the boards with a chevron pattern so you can reassemble them in order.

You can use the shooting board described above in a variation on its normal function, to prepare consistently angled edges ready for coopering. Place a shim under the far edge of the strip to lift it a little so the edge is tilted against the plane. Trial and error or scale drawing will lead you to the correct shim thickness to produce the desired radius of curvature. As when butt jointing flat boards, hold the strips together in front of a light so you can check if there are any gaps before gluing.

Pulling the angled edges together for gluing can be tricky unless you make a former of the right curvature to hold them in position without buckling. Now you need to apply an even clamping force at an angle. The best device I know of for this is the band cramp – effectively it is a mechanism for tensioning a length of webbing so it will pull at any angle.

When the glue on the coopered panel has set, you can plane the corners off the outside with a finely set smoothing plane. Keep working at the surface until you produce a continuous convex curve. The inside is trickier because it cannot be shaped with a flat-soled plane. You need to use one that has a sole that is convex when looked at endways. I use modified wooden block planes for this job; they are cheaply obtainable second-hand, the sole can be shaped with another plane, and the cutter ground in a matching curve.

5 The angled joints are planed to form a continuous curve.

6 A convex-soled plane smoothes inside the coopered panel.

7 The panel is rebated on a router table by using a straight cutter.

8 The rebated edge is cleaned up with a fine shoulder plane.

EDGE REBATES

After shaping the panel, its edge is rebated on a router table ready to fit in a groove in the sides of the box. A straight router cutter is fitted into the machine under the table and adjusted to protrude $3/16$in (5mm) above the table. The table's guide fence is positioned so that the front of the cutting edge is about $5/16$in (8mm) in front of the fence.

The straight edges of the panel are rebated simply by running them along the fence from right to left over the cutter. To cut rebates on the curved edges, the panel is laid on the table and the edge pressed against the fence. Rock the panel slowly while sliding it over the cutter, so that the line of contact between the curved underside and the table is always directly above the cutter. It may take several passes to produce a curved rebated edge with a consistent thickness. After routing, clean up the rebate to remove any wooliness with a fine shoulder plane.

CURVED GROOVE

Having prepared the boards that will form the sides of the box, a curved groove must be cut in each board to accept the rebated edge of the lid panel. The best technique for this is to use a handheld router, tethered to a pivot, so that it can only move in an arc. The radius must match that of a coopered panel and once again, geometry, drawing or trial and error will tell you the distance between router cutter and pivot point. Ensure there is no slack in the pivot arrangement – I drilled a hole in the metal plate of the router's sliding fence, then used the same drill shaft as a pivot pin.

All grooves need to be stopped short of the edge of the board so they will not be visible on the outside of the finished box. As with a flat panel, the coopered panel must be allowed to expand and contract across the grain with changes in seasonal humidity. The slot in the front and rear box panels needs extra depth to allow this movement; this means creating a gap between the outside edge of the panel and the inside of the groove, and a gap between the rebated edge and the inside of the frame. The movement could be as much as 2%, so allow 1% clearance on each side.

Straight grooves are needed in the front and rear of the box to accept the rebated edges of the panel. Although these panel edges are straight, they are inclined at an angle, so the groove needs to be cut at a corresponding angle to allow the edge to move in and out without causing gaps. I used the router table for this with a spacer bar clamped on top, parallel to the fence. This bar tilts the board at the appropriate angle for grooving.

9

10

11

9 A curved groove is cut with the router tethered to a pivot point.

10 The rebated edge of the coopered panel fits in the curved groove.

11 A spacer tilts the boards on the router table to make angled grooves.

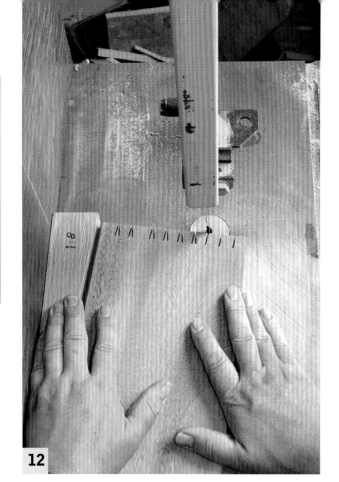

DOVETAILS

The finest way of cutting dovetails is the hand-sawn method because it allows you to make the tails extremely thin, however, it is also the slowest method. A quicker variation is to use a bandsaw instead of a dovetail saw.

The tails are marked out – but this time they are sawn by sliding them across the bandsaw table at an angle to the blade. Make a jig to keep the constant 1:8 angle used for hardwood dovetails from a wedge cut with a 1:8 ratio between side and end; next place it between the bandsaw fence and the board. Both the jig and the board must be slid together against the fence while making the cut.

Having sawn the tail sides, the sockets are chopped out and pared back to the shoulder line. You can make the waste easier to remove with a chisel by first making intermediate bandsaw cuts into it. The dovetail pins are marked on to the edge of the corresponding board using the freshly cut

tails as a template. The board is tilted while being fed straight into the bandsaw blade. The pin sides are cut above the bandsaw table with the board supported at a 1:8 angle.

It is important that the wood must be well supported above the table, otherwise the normally well-behaved bandsaw can snatch viciously. To provide this support you will need a large wedge shaped surface, like a slab of cheese resting on its side on the table. Finally the waste is removed from the sockets located between pins, and the joints can be trial fitted partway, taking great care not to jam them together.

12 To bandsaw dovetail tails, a narrow wedge alongside the fence locates the board at the correct angle.

13 The sockets between tails are chopped out with a fine bevel-edged chisel.

14 To bandsaw dovetail pins, a wide wedge underneath tilts the board.

ONE-PIECE BOX

I find it is best to assemble and glue up dovetailed boxes complete with the top and bottom panels trapped in slots, then separate the lid from the base with a saw after the glue has set, and the outer surfaces have been planed. This avoids any risk of mismatch between the two halves of the box.

Of course, the process of sawing must be carried out with great care, as by this stage you will have invested a lot of effort in the construction. In anticipation of this stage, when you lay out the dovetails for a box, allow extra spacing between the pins at the height where you will saw the lid from the base, including enough to plane the edges true.

HINGING

Position a pair of brass butt hinges so that the centre line of the pin is just outside the back of the box and lid. Before cutting a rebate to let the hinge plate into, fix each hinge temporarily to the surface. Use steel screws at first rather than brass ones, which are easily damaged. This will allow you to confirm the position and ensure the lid closes in good alignment, before marking around the hinge plates with a knife line.

The router is very effective for levelling out the base of a hinge rebate. Rather than setting up a template, I find it best to rout freehand, leaving a margin around the edges to be chopped away later with a chisel. Brass hinges can be polished with wet and dry paper or fine steel wool then metal polish, but this is best done after the hinges have been test fitted and removed to avoid scratching the metal or contaminating the wood. After initial fitting, the steel screws can be exchanged for brass screws of the same size and the threads lubricated by wax.

15 After the glue has set, the lid is sawn off the box.

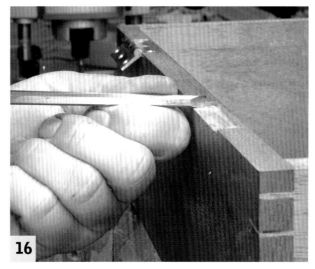

16 Rebates for hinges are routed freehand then trimmed with a chisel.

17 Check the lid alignment before sanding and polishing.

Veneered table

   Skill level 3 | Machinery used: bandsaw

This tall occasional table uses solid walnut legs and frame, with secret mitre dovetails (see page 60) at the corners to support a top made with bandsawn veneers (see page 104) of walnut.

ABOVE This tall, minimal table has legs and frame constructed from solid walnut and a veneered top.

The advantage the veneered table top has over solid wood is that it will not move with changing moisture content. While a solid-wood table top must be constructed and fixed so the width can expand and shrink in response to humidity variations, this top has the frame firmly bonded to its outer edge, adding visual depth and giving the table a monolithic appearance.

THICKNESS

Commercial veneers are knife-cut extremely thinly, obviously to give a high yield from valuable timbers, but also because this helps the machine to peel the fresh-cut veneer away from the wetted log without cracking. The consequence for the furniture-maker is that the veneers are frequently buckled and fragile to handle. It is impractical to plane a surface incorporating commercial veneer – after a few strokes, you will start to see through it. The finished furniture can look good but with time and wear, the thin surface is susceptible to damage or blistering with damp heat. Bandsawn veneers are typically cut to around $\frac{1}{16}$in (1.5–2mm) making them thick enough to handle and plane, but not thick enough for wood movement to cause problems.

BANDSAW VENEER

You will need to slice enough veneer on the bandsaw to cover both sides of the table top. The balancing veneer on the underside will resist the pull caused by shrinkage of the face veneer as it dries. When choosing timbers suitable for veneering a table top, you are free from worrying about the structure and can concentrate on the aesthetics – a busy, lively figuring or calm, mild grain will be equally functional. Use a timber that is thick enough to provide all the pieces needed for one face, that way the colours will match and you can produce a coordinated pattern from the figuring.

Having set up the bandsaw with a fresh skip-tooth blade and a rigid high-sided fence, adjust for drift and brace the fence to the upper guide. The thickness can be adjusted within by very tiny amounts. Cut the veneers, planing a fresh surface on the timber before each pass of the bandsaw, so the veneer comes off with one smooth face and one sawn face.

Veneers need edge jointing so they will butt together with a near invisible line. The best way to achieve this is with a variation on the shooting-board technique. Clamp the veneer between two straight-edged pieces of manufactured board, so the veneer protrudes by less than a millimetre. Lay a long-soled plane on its side and run it along the edge of the veneer, carefully trimming back along to the board.

PREPARING THE GROUND

Engineered wood products such as MDF, make a suitable substrate for veneering because they have negligible movement with humidity, hence they will not strain when bonded directly to the long grain of an outer frame. The board must be completely flat and thick enough to stay that way. Personal protection from a breathing mask and goggles are needed when working with MDF, because of the formaldehyde released.

1 Veneers for the table top are bandsawn from a board of walnut.

Gap-filling resin adhesive is ideal for laying veneer that has a saw-marked rear surface. Alternatively, PVA will do the job, but the contact will not be complete, consequently the adhesion not as strong. Make up enough glue to coat both surfaces of the board, as the backing veneer should ideally be applied at the same time. The glue is rolled onto the ground board using a hard, rubber roller. Soft rollers meant for paint will do the job, but they soak up glue and waste it, and then they need washing out or throwing away.

The sheets of veneer are laid out in order on the surface that will become the underside of the ground. The veneer tends to cup away from the

2

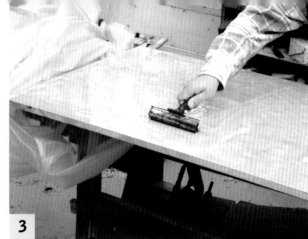

3

4

5

2 Clamped between a pair of MDF sheets in a shooting board arrangement, the edges of the veneer are 'jointed'.

3 Gap-filling resin adhesive is rolled onto the ground board.

4 The sheets of veneer are laid in order on both sides of the groundwork or substrate.

5 With the table top inside the vacuum press bag, the vacuum pump does its work.

board on first contact, as the underside absorbs moisture from the glue. All the sheets are butted together and taped, to stop the freshly glued veneers peeling off when the board is turned over. Veneering tape is designed to pull itself tighter when moist although masking tape will do the job. The upper side of the ground is veneered with walnut showing the best figuring, then the vacuum bag is pulled into place over the board. You may need to borrow an extra pair of hands for this operation.

With the table top inside the vacuum press bag, the seals are closed, the vacuum pump connected by rigid hose and the pump switched on. The pump extracts air from the bag and within a couple of minutes, the bag will apply nearly full atmospheric pressure to the wood. I say 'nearly' full atmospheric pressure to emphasize the point that this process does not require a particularly high vacuum. If, for example, the pump were to leave 10% of the air behind – which would be a pretty weak vacuum pump – there would still be 90% of the pressure on the wood in the bag, which is a substantial nine tonnes per square metre (0.9 tons per square foot). To ensure there is no gross leakage, you can switch the pump off and check that the bag stays taut for several seconds before switching back on again. Note that some pumps will not re-start with a vacuum on the inlet so it may be necessary to bleed air into the tube before re-starting.

FRAMEWORK

The framework around the table top is made from solid walnut, finished at $^{15}/_{16}$in (24mm) thick and grooved to take the rebated edge of the veneered board. The corner joints are externally mitred with an internal lapped dovetail, known as secret mitred dovetail (see page 60 for instructions). Simple mitred joints with ends cut at 45° would look tidy but have very little strength, because the glue would be trying to adhere end grain-to-end grain. By incorporating a three-quarter thickness dovetail inside the joint, it gains mechanical strength as well as a large internal area of long grain-to-long grain contact for the glue to bond.

Crosscut the boards to length before face planing and edging them, then thicknessing. If you get your timber supplier to do the thicknessing for you, then it is advisable to have them do it in the same order so that any minor curvature along the full length of the uncut board will not limit the thickness of the finished boards. All four sides of the frame must be of equal thickness for the mitres to work.

FRAME THE TOP

The veneered table top must be rebated to leave a tongue to fit into the slotted frame. Use a router to remove the bulk of the material then finish the rebate with a shoulder plane to restore the straight, smooth edge on the veneer.

With all the secret mitre dovetail joints prepared, the four sides of the frame must be grooved to receive the edges of the table top. This can be done with a plough plane or a router. The groove must be positioned at such a height that the table top will end up almost level with the top edges of the frame, allowing a little extra height on the frame, so it can be planed flush after gluing.

6 Walnut boards are cut to length ready to face and edge.

7 Rebate the veneered table-top edge to fit in the slotted frame.

8 The table-top frame is fitted to the table top.

Bandsawn veneers have sufficient thickness to allow them to be planed as part of the levelling operation. However, you need to be careful that the grain direction may conflict when planing veneer alongside the frame, causing one side of the plane to cut smoothly, while the other catches and tears at the surface. This process will be more forgiving if the plane blade is razor sharp, and you may need to angle the plane so the blade takes a shearing action across the conflicting grain, rather than challenging it head-on.

9

10

HOLLOW LEGS

The removable legs are made from solid walnut boards, butt-jointed edge-to-face in a tubular square section around a hollow centre. When the table top frame is stood on its legs, the boards forming the outside faces of the legs are butted against the underside of the table top frame, so they carry its weight. The boards forming the inside faces are taller and continue up inside the table top frame so they can be bolted onto it. Long horizontal holes are bored edgewise through the width of the rear leg boards to take steel bolts. I used tapped studding rods and nuts to make suitable length bolts. The bolts are passed through the holes then driven into cross-dowels, sunk in vertical holes drilled in the underside of the table top frame. These secure the legs to the frame, keeping the wooden faces of the components pressed tightly in alignment.

11

9 The table top frame is planed flush.

10 Legs are constructed from boards butt-jointed edge-to-face.

11 Holes drilled edgewise, through the inside leg boards, take the fixing bolts.

12

FINISHING

All the outside edges are chamfered with a hand held block plane to remove the sharp arrises. This also creates a visible joint line between legs and frame, without which the slightest misalignment would show when the legs were bolted to the frame.

The clients for my table wanted to stand drinks on the top without worrying about marking; that meant using a tough synthetic finish over the wood. I chose to use water-borne acrylic varnish, which is sold as the toughest surface finish for protecting floorboards. The varnish can be applied by brush, but it gives a better, smoother finish when applied with a spray gun. I use a high-volume low pressure (HVLP) spray system, which places more of the varnish on the wood, and leaves less as a mist in the air than the high-pressure type.

Rub the components of the table along the grain with medium-grade abrasive paper before applying finish, then with fine-grade paper to de-nib between coats. Once the final coat has set, any slight roughness can be removed with 0000 grade steel wool to give the finish a nice, silky touch. Lubricate the steel wool with wax paste polish on a gloss finish, or with Vaseline jelly on a semi-matt finish.

The table I made was over 39½in (1m) tall for a client who wanted to stand in front of a high window with a view of hills and countryside. This

13

14

12 Cross-dowels are sunk into holes in the underside of the table-top frame.

13 The finished legs are offered up to the inside of the table-top frame, then bolted in place.

14 Wing-nuts inside secure the legs against the frame.

is twice the height of a typical coffee table while dining tables typically have a height of 28½in (724mm). However, the simple square tubular legs of this design can easily be adapted to any height.

Demilune table

 Skill level 3 | Machinery used: bandsaw

This project uses two variations on the techniques of laminating (see pages 100–103 for more details on laminating), together with mortice and tenon joints and butt joints, to produce a simple but elegant piece of furniture.

ABOVE The finished table's classical roots and simple clean lines give it a contemporary feel.

We have looked at the theory and methods of laminating as a means of producing components that are curved to pre-defined shapes, while retaining the character and figuring of solid wood (see pages 100–103). The hall table borrows the principle of its curved shape top and apron from designs of the early 1800s when 'demilunes' were fashionable in well-to-do European households. With its simple clean lines and semi-elliptical top, shallower than the conventional crescent shape, this interpretation of the demilune stands comfortably in a contemporary interior.

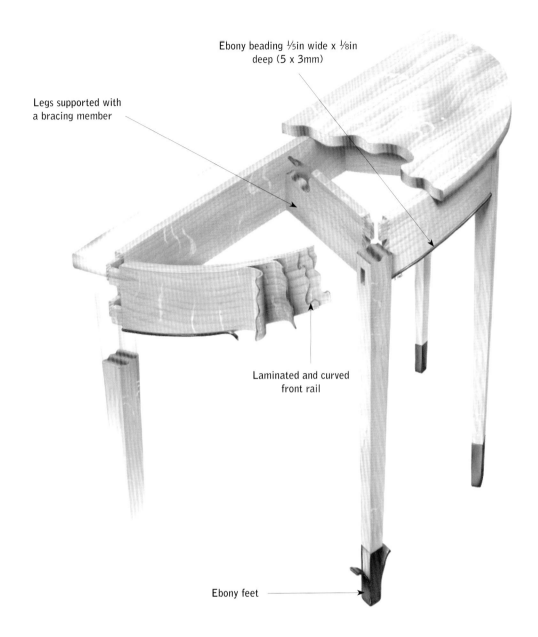

Ebony beading ⅕in wide x ⅛in deep (5 x 3mm)

Legs supported with a bracing member

Laminated and curved front rail

Ebony feet

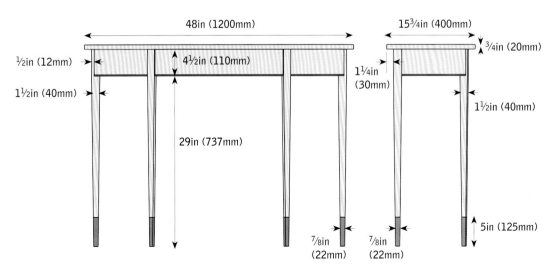

48in (1200mm)

15¾in (400mm)

½in (12mm)

4½in (110mm)

¾in (20mm)

1½in (40mm)

1¼in (30mm)

1½in (40mm)

29in (737mm)

5in (125mm)

⅞in (22mm)

⅞in (22mm)

DEMILUNE TABLE   **169**

CONTRASTING WOODS

Used in moderation, contrasting woods work well together. Ebony (*Diospurus sp*) and oak (*Quercus sp*) could not be more different from one another, both in their appearance and nature. African ebony is dense, black and hard, with a grain that is often invisible to the naked eye. Indian varieties and others from around the Indian Ocean such as Macassar ebony, include dark brown streaks. Nowadays, furniture-makers use ebony in small quantities, both because of the need to conserve the tropical environment and because coming from small trees, ebony has always been an expensive wood. The ebony I used was pure black in colour, and I bought it prepared in two ways – roughly sawn rectangular blocks from which I cut thick veneer slabs to make the sabots (wooden shoes), and long, thin knife-cut strips from which I laminated the beaded edge under the apron. European oak has a golden colour and a clearly visible grain structure.

BOARDS

Boards that have been sawn radially along the trunk, so the growth rings run at right angles to the faces, will show a medullary ray pattern or 'silver grain' that is a special characteristic of oak. Not only does this look attractive but it also guarantees minimal distortion with changes in seasonal humidity – a particular concern for furniture-makers constructing large flat surfaces like table tops. Timber converters can produce quantities of oak like this by quarter-sawing, but this is skilful and labour-intensive work, which produces wasteful offcuts. Consequently, most modern timber is flat-sawn. However, by selecting only the widest boards sawn through the centre of the trunk, furniture-makers can obtain oak that is essentially the same as the best quarter-sawn. It will have the same medullary ray pattern as quarter-sawn oak.

The top must not include any sapwood or shakes (cracks) from the heart of the trunk, so it will almost certainly need an edge joint or butt joint to make it wide enough. If possible, arrange this joint so it is between edges from the outside of the tree – that way the front and back edges will be of the hardest heartwood from the centre of the tree. This makes them more durable and cleaner to cut. If the top is to be made from flat-sawn boards showing long, curved tree rings, you should try to alternate the ring direction to cancel out a tendency to bow.

ELLIPTICAL CURVE

Use a piece of white hardboard or thin MDF as a rod or pattern to mark out the elliptical shape of the top and the apron rails beneath. The easiest way

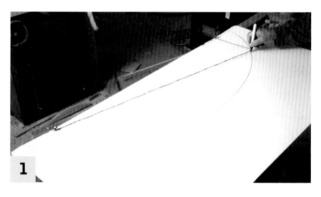

3

to produce a semi-ellipse is to use a pencil to stretch a slack string secured between two map-pins. Play around with pin spacing and string length until you produce the size and shape of ellipse you want. Increasing the distance between the pins will increase the major axis and reduce the minor axis, while increasing the amount of slack in the string increases both the major and minor axis.

Cut the shape of the oak top oversize with a bandsaw or jigsaw. After surface-planing and thicknessing, edge joint them as near invisibly as possible. The completed table top can then be bandsawn accurately up to the curved edge line, ready for hand planing. Now you will need to fair the elliptical edge into a smooth, continuous curve. You might use a compass plane as I did, following the ellipse as a series of small arcs, and continuously adjusting the radius control on the plane sole as you move round to the next arc. Alternatively, use a flat-soled spokeshave, which is a more versatile and considerably cheaper tool for fairing curves, but

1 The semi-ellipse is drawn on hardboard using a slack string between two map pins.

2 After rough sawing and butt jointing, the top is faired with a compass plane.

3 Using a convex spokeshave, the curve is given a barrel edge.

4 Legs are tapered with a series of progressively longer plane strokes.

one which takes more care and practice for good results. Having established a true and smooth elliptical edge with the compass plane, I gave the curve a second dimension – a barrel edge – using a convex spokeshave. Again, a flat-soled spokeshave can be used.

TAPERED LEGS

The legs are 33½in (850mm) long overall, making the demilune higher than dining tables, which are normally 28½in (724mm) high. The extra height is more suitable for a hall table, which people will walk past rather than sit at. It also makes the legs appear more slender and elegant. They start to taper on three faces from the base of the rails, and finish at the feet with tapered ebony feet or sabots made from bandsawn lippings.

The legs are square-sectioned all the way down, 1½in (40mm) at the level of the rails, and ⅞in (22mm) at the base of the foot. The fourth face, which forms the front of the front legs and the outsides of the back legs, has a flat surface from end to end – when the frame is assembled, these outer faces stand vertical so as the legs appear slightly splayed even though they are not. The legs are sawn to shape, then surface planed, before the recesses to take the ebony lippings are cut on the bandsaw.

4

FITTING THE EBONY FEET

The ebony I used for the feet came from a 1in (25mm) wide billet. After smoothing one face of the ebony with a block plane, use the bandsaw with a fine-toothed blade to cut the ebony to about about ⅛in (3mm) thickness. Then repeat the planing and sawing for each slice (16 in total). Don't cut the ebony too thin or it will be delicate and curl when you glue it, and you need thickness to allow for chamfering the edges. Glue up one opposite pair of ebony lippings at a time with as many cramps as you can fit. When set, cut the other pair to a fine fit, glue up, then finely plane the legs end-to-end.

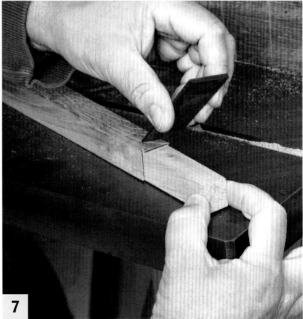

5 Feet have their faces sawn off to provide a housing for the ebony.

6 A set of 16 ebony veneers – each one is surface planed and bandsawn off the block.

7 The ebony fits in the sabot housings.

8 The laminations are glued up between matching formers.

9 Ebony strips are laminated on the lower edge of the oak apron.

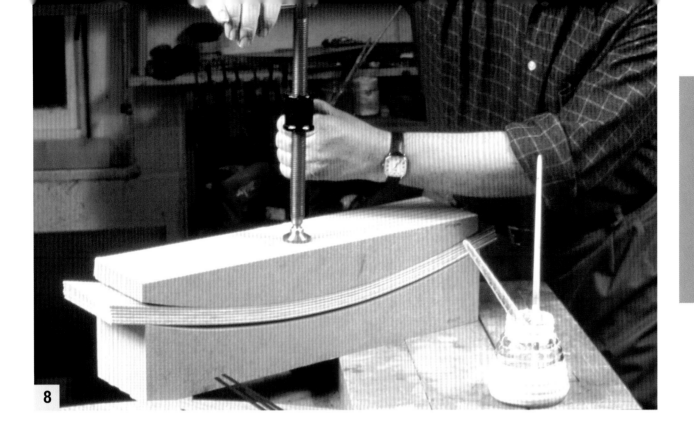

8

APRON RAILS

Each curved front rail is laminated to its own shape
to make up part of the semi-ellipse. The shape of the
rails is marked out on the underside of the table top
1⅛in (30mm) from the edge, using a pencil marker
gauge. This is used as a guide to the shape of the
formers for shaping the laminated rail sections while
they set. Two sets of matching formers are needed,
one symmetrical set for the middle and another
asymmetrical set which can be used for both sides.
The shape is marked on the hardboard rod by
drawing a line approximately 1⅝in (40mm) in
from the table top edge, along with the positions
and angles of the legs and joints. The formers are
bandsawn from sheets of MDF then glued together.
Surfaces are smoothed to stop them marking the oak.

There is a moderate amount of tension trapped
in laminated woodwork, so it tends to open out
slightly when it is released. This means the formers
need a slightly tighter curvature than the finished
components. Prepare oak on the bandsaw ready for
laminating the rails. Allow extra length that you
can cut off to make tidy ends ready for cutting the
tenons. You can use a gap-filling glue to bond the
rough-sawn laminations because the only edge that
shows will be on the underside. Once the formers
and laminations have been pulled together with a
couple of cramps, grab as many cramps as you can
fit, to apply even, firm, pressure while the glue sets.

MAKING THE EBONY BEADING

With three curved oak rails formed, the edges
planed and tenons cut on the ends, the next stage is
running a curved ebony beading around the lower
rail edges. This calls for a bit of micro-laminating.

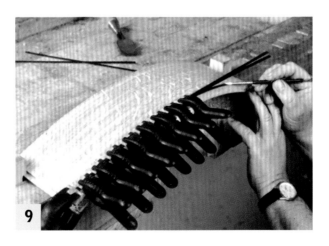

9

The finished bead will be ¼in (6mm) wide by ⅛in (3mm) deep. Ebony is brittle and it does not take kindly to being bent, so the beading is built up of three ³⁄₆₄in (1mm) thick laminations before shaping. These laminations, unlike the rails, would show any glue lines rather badly, so they need good, flat faces for gluing. Having prepared and cut three lengths of stringing for each piece of bead – nine in total – progressively glue them onto the curved lower edge of each piece of rail, clamping in place continuously as you work your way along.

SCRATCH STOCK

Scratch stocks are described on page 39 and now we will use this simple tool to shape the round edge on the bead after the glue has set. To make a suitable scratch stock, take a short piece of hacksaw blade, say 1¼in (30mm) long, file off the teeth, and grind the faces and edges flat and smooth. Make up a concave cutting edge by filing a ¼in (6mm) diameter semicircular notch, ⅛in (3mm) deep, in one edge of the piece of blade. Try to give the inside cutting edge a finely ground inner surface, square to the faces and sharp, square edges.

Make a square hardwood shaft to fit in a basic joiner's marking gauge, and cut a fine saw-slot in one end about 2in (50mm) long to hold the blade. Carve a semicircular groove across the shaft, slightly larger than the notch in the blade. Place the blade in the slot, making sure the straight edge of the blade is slightly recessed so it cannot mark the curved surface of the oak rails. Pinch it in place by tightening the thumbscrew, and the scratch stock is ready for use.

Ebony responds well to scraping and if the tool edge is fine, the ebony surface will cut to a sheen straight from the blade. Patience is a virtue in using this type of tool, many light passes are best – sneak up on the required shape rather than trying to force it. A touch of beeswax on the tool helps keep it moving with a light touch and no judder. Use a dry

10

brush and vacuum to remove fine ebony scrapings as you go along so they don't find their way into the open oak pores.

UNDER FRAME

Each leg has a sturdy bracing member to support it. This is provided by a ²⁵⁄₃₂in (20mm) thick rail across the back of the table, tenoned to the inside of each back leg. Two radial rails are tenoned into each of the front legs and doweled into the back rail. Dowels are popular with some furniture-makers, while others have a low opinion of them. I think this is because they were used wrongly by mass producers in the middle of the last century, sometimes resulting in shoddy furniture when the dowels were over-stressed. In suitable joints like this, dowels permit the exact alignment to be marked during a dry fit.

With the legs and frame rigidly assembled, the top is fitted using L-shaped buttons screwed to the top and dry-tenoned into the frame, just as we did for the elm cabinet.

10 The ebony beading is shaped with a scratch stock.

11 Angled cross rails are fixed to the back rail with dowels.

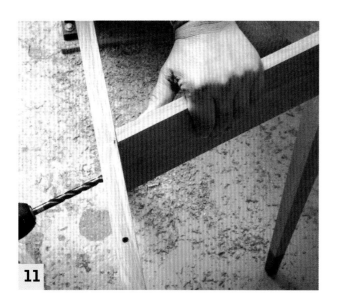

FINISHING

By hand planing all the components with a fine-set blade before assembly, very little is needed in the way of sanding to give the surfaces a silky touch. The legs need to have micro-chamfers down each corner or 'arris' to prevent splinters forming. You may also wish to wax the components but take care not to get any on glue surfaces. A simple wax finish with beeswax/carnauba paste provides a light sheen and some protection, keeping the colours fresh and the grain open. Avoid using steel wool on light oak as it can trap metal particles producing microscopic black iron/tannin stains.

This table is simple in the sense that it does not use a great many components, but it does call upon many techniques. It also requires a great deal of care and patience in marking out and cutting the correctly angled joints. However, you will be rewarded with a fine piece of furniture to exhibit your skills.

12 Buttons are dry-morticed into rails and screwed to the table top to allow seasonal movement.

13 All the edges of the finished table are chamfered with a fine plane.

14 Micro-chamfers keep the edges crisp, yet smooth to touch.

Set of dining chairs

   Skill level 3 | Machinery used: bandsaw

Practise the shaping, curving and angling skills learnt on pages 108–113 with this pleasing set of dining chairs that incorporate armrests into each one for added comfort and strength.

Carvers, or dining chairs with armrests, are frequently supplied in pairs with the remainder of the set having no armrests. In these egalitarian days this seems unfair as most people prefer to use dining chairs with armrests, so this projects is a set of four carvers. Apart from the obvious function of providing somewhere to rest your arms during a relaxing meal, the armrests offer additional support while you sit or stand as well as being handles for lifting and moving the chairs. From the maker's point of view, armrests on dining chairs provide additional bracing, removing the need for rails beneath the seat. In my view, this makes carvers a more satisfactory construction than their armless equivalents.

ECONOMY OF SCALE

Sets of chairs provide the maker and the buyer with some economies of scale compared to a single item of furniture. While the chairs are still individually made, the processes of using templates to make identical parts, repeated measurements and angles for the joints and repeated setups for simple jigs all reduce the making time per chair. Making a set of four chairs, or half a dozen, is by no means mass production but there is some satisfaction to be gained from the repeated methods and the planning involved that improve the efficiency of the processes. There is also some economy in the use of materials gained from nesting the cut-out patterns for curved chair components from one inside another.

LEFT A set of carver dining chairs in brown oak.

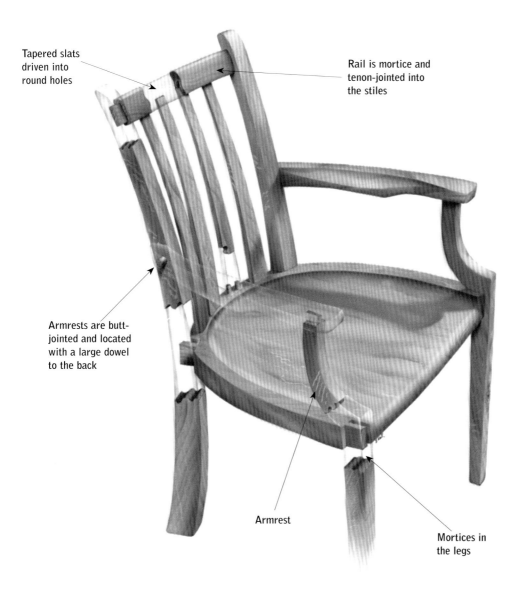

Tapered slats driven into round holes

Rail is mortice and tenon-jointed into the stiles

Armrests are butt-jointed and located with a large dowel to the back

Armrest

Mortices in the legs

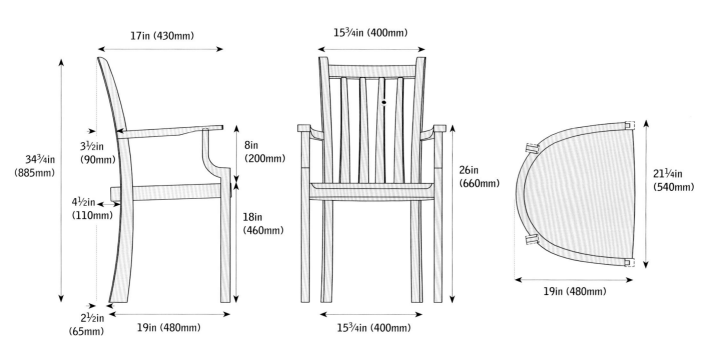

17in (430mm)

15¾in (400mm)

34¾in (885mm)

3½in (90mm)

8in (200mm)

4½in (110mm)

26in (660mm)

18in (460mm)

21¼in (540mm)

2½in (65mm)

19in (480mm)

15¾in (400mm)

19in (480mm)

SET OF DINING CHAIRS **177**

BROWN OAK

The wood used for this project is brown oak, sawn to a nominal 2in (50mm) thickness and air-dried, then kilned. Golden oak or other coarse-grained native hardwoods such as ash or elm would be suitable. Excessive seasonal movement in a wide wooden seat like the ones made for these chairs could seriously distort the chair and weaken the joints. The moisture content needs to be stable at around 10%–12% for equilibrium with the air in a dry, warm house. Using thick timber such as this means changes in moisture content are slow. It has the advantage that the finished chair will be less responsive to short-term seasonal changes but the disadvantage that you need to wait longer to ensure the wood is acclimatized to the workshop before cutting it.

MAKING THE SEATS

The brown oak is sawn into short butts and the solid seats are made from three of these butts edge-jointed together to make the required width. Edges are jointed in the same way as we have previously used, by hand planing pairs of edges clamped together. Because the width of a pair of edges is approaching 4in (100mm), the jointer plane, which is much narrower, must be angled so that the sole sits flat across the pair of edges.

The edges are pressed together dry and checked with a desk lamp behind to make sure there is no chink of light sneaking through, especially towards the edge ends where the plane could easily dip by accident. The seats are then glued up by using a modern waterproof PVA type adhesive that forms cross-link bonds and would not be weakened by any accidental spillages. Sash cramps are used to hold the joints together.

1 The brown oak is sawn into short butts.

2 Edges are jointed.

3 The seats are glued up.

BANDSAW SHAPING

Templates for the U-shaped seat include the tenon joints for the legs to be fixed on to the four corners. I find it best to cut the outline of the seat first on the bandsaw, leaving plenty of excess around each joint, returning later to fine-tune the joint shapes and angles on the bandsaw, with the assistance of some sharp chisels.

The legs, arms and rails are also bandsawn from the solid 2in (50mm) thick material, 'nesting' similarly shaped parts inside one another to avoid excess wastage and make best use of the timber. After bandsawing, the components are all trimmed back to the shape of the template using the router table or spindle-moulder technique. The mortices in the legs are chopped then tried and adjusted to fit the tenons on the seat corners at an early stage to ensure all the components are viable before moving on to shaping the seat tops.

4 Tenon joints cut on the bandsaw.

5 A complete set of seats cut on the bandsaw.

6 Some economy of materials is gained by 'nesting' parts.

7 Joints are trimmed and tried at an early stage.

DISHING THE SEATS

The seats for these chairs are shaped from the solid to form gently curved hollows with tightly curved edges. Make this shape in two stages. First rout the tightly curved channel around the edge using a large round cutter. Next hollow out the main area using a rotary carver (which is a steel disk surrounded by chainsaw-type teeth) with a guided motion to remove the bulk material, as I will explain below.

A template made from MDF or ply, being the same shape as the seat but considerably smaller, is used to guide the router as it forms a round-bottomed groove inside the edges of the seats. The router cutter has a 1in (25mm) radius, which is about as large as I care to use in a handheld router. Make the groove in a series of shallower cuts so there is no risk of the machine being dragged off course.

A SWINGING CUTTER

With the routed groove forming a channel around the outside of the seat, position and clamp the seat on the workbench beneath a beam or secure hook, some 78in (2000mm) above. A wire rope (I used a length of plastic-covered steel washing line) is passed over the beam or a suitable hook, and looped around the spindle guard of a rotary carver, fitted in an angle-grinder motor. The ends of the steel rope can be raised or lowered, then clamped onto the bench to fix the height of the cutter disk.

9

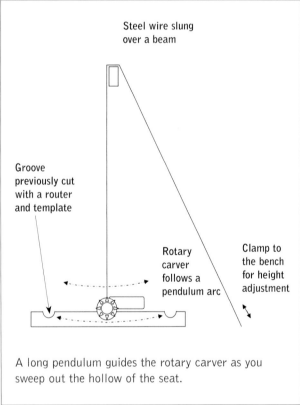

Steel wire slung over a beam

Groove previously cut with a router and template

Rotary carver follows a pendulum arc

Clamp to the bench for height adjustment

A long pendulum guides the rotary carver as you sweep out the hollow of the seat.

8

8 Using a template to route the tight radius groove around the edge of the seat dish.

9 A long, sweeping pendulum guides the rotary carver.

Use this system to guide the movement of the rotary carver as you sweep it in a 78in (2000mm) radius arc, forming the hollowed-out base of the seat. Particular care is needed at the end of each sweep as you want the arc of the rotary carver cut to blend into the groove previously cut with the large-radius router. The pendulum will, of course, swing fore and aft as well as side to side, producing a hollow curved in both directions. I recommend practising this technique on scrap before taking risks with expensive and carefully prepared wood.

SMOOTHING THE HOLLOW

Having used the router and rotary carver to hollow out the seat, you will need to further shape and smooth the sitting surface. This could be done with a chair-makers' travisher or a convex spokeshave, but I prefer to use a wooden plane that I have shaped to be convex in both directions. Old wooden planes are readily available from junk-shops or internet auctions. With the blade removed, the shape of the sole can be shaped with a block plane. The blade then needs grinding to a corresponding curve before you re-fit it.

10 Home-shaped planes finish the seat dishing.

11 A complete kit of parts ready for assembling the chairs.

NUMBERING PARTS

In making a set of chairs, you will build up a surprisingly large number of parts. Ideally, these might all be interchangeable, but in practice there are two considerations preventing this: firstly, you will probably fine-tune the fitting of individual joints; secondly, you will want to match parts for appearance so the colouring and figuring are consistent on each chair. This means numbering the parts as you check their fit A1, A2, B1, B2 etc. It is necessary to number on places that will not be shaved or sanded off during the shaping processes, such as the undersides of feet or the cheeks of tenons.

10

11

BACK CONSTRUCTION

The backs of these dining chairs have a top rail fitted between the back legs or 'stiles' and a set of tapered slats running between the rail and the seat. The rail needs to be carefully mortice and tenon-jointed into the stiles at the correct angle and length. I used the double-ended angle gauge to make this fit.

The slats are tapered at the top and driven into round holes bored into the underside of the rails. The wide lower ends are fixed to the seat by pegs, like long dowels, driven through the holes in the seat into corresponding holes in the ends of the slats.

12 The slats are fixed at the lower end by long pegs driven through the seat

13 Seat and legs are pulled together by even pressure from band-cramps.

GLUE UP THE FRAME

The seats and legs are glued up and pulled together with band-cramps which apply some considerable pressure without distorting the shape of the chair. The front legs are curved from front to back and tapered on the inside to support the arms above the seat level.

The armrests will be used for lifting these heavy chairs, so it is important their joints are not prone to working loose. While the armrest supports on top of the front legs need to be moderately thin, the tenon joints on top of them should be as large as possible. I made them 1in (25mm) square which is the full section of the wood at this point, without a shoulder. Wedges are fitted in a pair of slots within each tenon (fox wedges) and these are pressed into place as the joint is driven together, making a secure fit.

12

13

FINISHING

As with most furniture, it is normal to shape and prepare the surfaces of components for chairs before joining and gluing them together. Having fitted all the parts together there will be further sanding required which can be done with a random orbit power tool or by hand following the direction of the wood grain. The edges are all chamfered, either with a wide chamfer, which forms part of the shaping, or an edge chamfer, which provides a smooth splinter-free line and catches the light.

The surfaces of chairs are inevitably subject to wear through contact with clothes and hands, while dining chairs may be subject to spillages as well. The options to cope with this are either to make the surface finish so thick and impervious that it is practically indestructible, or to use an oil finish that can be supplemented and maintained over the years. The latter option provides a more friendly 'woody' as opposed to 'plastic' finish, so I would encourage clients to choose this.

Apply Danish oil generously to all surfaces then wipe off with a dry cotton rag after about 20 minutes, before the oil has a chance to coagulate on the surface. When the first coat has dried after a day or two, the grain will be rough and need de-nibbing again with fine sandpaper. A further two or three coats of oil over the following week will bring the chairs to a good satin finish.

14 Armrest tenons are unshouldered and fox-wedged to prevent joints loosening.

15 The dished seat and tapered parts give more finesse to the heavy construction.

14

15

Glossary (US terms in brackets)

air-dried converted by removing water with natural ventilation

anemometer meter to measure air speed, used for checking dust extractors

arbor spindle or axle on which a machine blade turns

Arbortech rotary carver or toothed disk for rapid wood removal, attached to an angle-grinder

arris long, sharp corner where face of a board meets the edge

Bailey hand plane, commonest type for smoothing with depth adjustor under back of blade

Bedrock version of a Bailey hand plane with improved frog fixings

biscuit beech-wood segment pressed in pair of slots to form a rapid joint

blast gate air valve used to control flow from machines to an extractor

block plane small hand-plane without frog used for trimming

bowed board curved from end to end, usually due to tension in the tree

bridge guard protection shield over cutter block of surface planer (jointer)

bridle joint open-sided mortice and tenon or slot joint

bull-nose hand plane with blade near front end, or half-round edge on table top etc

burnisher steel rod used to flatten scraper edges

burr (burl) knotty wood produced by excess twig growth, popular for veneers

case hardened voids inside board due to poor drying, 'honeycombing' revealed when sawn, can make board useless

caul semi-rigid mould or former used for pressing veneer

checks cracks visible on outside of a board due to poor drying conditions

contractor-saw lightweight circular saw table

cool-block metal block guides for bandsaw blades

cramp (clamp) portable screwed jaws for pressing pieces of wood together

crosscut cutting across the fibres (fibers) so they are severed

crown-sawn board converted by flitch sawing towards the edge of a log

cubic foot (twelve board-foot) common measure for buying wood. 35.3 cubic feet equals one cubic metre (meter)

cupped board curved from side to side due to uneven shrinkage

cutter block rotating cylinder holding the knives of a planer (jointer) or thicknesser (planer)

cutting gauge marker with a stock, stem and blade for scoring a fine line parallel to an edge

dimension saw sawbench with large arm for cutting sheet material, also called panel saw

domino rectangular beech-wood block pressed in pair of slot mortices to form a rapid joint

dovetail finger joint with tapered teeth, suited to drawers and boxes

dowel cylinder of wood pressed in pair of holes for a rapid joint

drift unintentional movement of sawblade away from the line

dust and chipping extractor type with impellor feeding filter above collecting bag

feed rate speed of wood fed into blades on a machine

ferrule metal ring often used to stop wood splitting

flitch cut board sawn from one side of trunk to the other

frog movable iron wedge on a hand plane that the blade is fixed to

glue line visible line after wood pieces are glued together

gullet gap between saw teeth

haunch extra part on tenon shoulder to prevent twisting

heartwood older growth towards middle of tree trunk, usually harder than sapwood

HEPA High Efficiency Particulate in Air filter, removes very fine dust

honing flattening the edge of a blade with fine abrasive

HSS High Speed Steel used for machine cutting tools that may run hot

inch thick (four quarter or 4/4) 25.40mm thick, common thickness for converted timber

kerf slot left by a sawblade

kickback wood thrown from machine when it catches on a blade

kiln-dried converted by removing water in a controlled warm enclosure

lamina thin slice used to form lamination when several are glued together

lapped dovetail (half-blind) recessed dovetail used for drawer fronts

machining (milling) initial sizing and smoothing to prepare wood for fine work

marking gauge marker with a stock, stem and pin for scoring line parallel to an edge

MDF Medium Density Fibreboard (Fiberboard) dense, uniform sheet manufactured from compressed wood particles

mitre sloping end or edge, can be paired to form a right angle

moisture content quantity of water in wood as a percentage of dry weight

mortice hole to receive a tenon and form a joint, usually rectangular

mortice gauge marker with block, stem and two independently moved pins for scoring a pair of lines parallel to an edge

muntin a vertical frame division

Norris hand plane with combined depth and level adjuster above blade

panel saw hand-saw for general use, also machine sawbench similar to dimension saw

paring slicing along the grain with a chisel

PCD Poly Crystalline Diamond, fine, hard abrasive used for long-life cutting edges

pistol grip saw handle with open underside

pitch distance between saw teeth etc

pith centre of tree trunk produced by first growth, often discarded

planer (jointer) machine for smoothing surface of timber

plywood composite manufactured board with thin layers of wood glued in alternate grain directions

PPE Personal Protection Equipment such as safety glasses, ear defenders, breathing masks

pressure pad block used to push wood over surface of a planer (jointer)

protractor angle-measuring gauge, often semicircular

push stick forked-end tool, normally wooden or plastic, for moving wood into a machine cutter without risk to hands

quarter-sawn stable boards produced by sawing at an angle close to the radius of the trunk

rake-angle angle of saw teeth to direction of blade movement

reaction wood wood distorted or patterned by stress in growing tree

re-saw cut boards thinner after they have been dried, also a specialist bandsaw for this job

rip-cut sawing along the grain direction

riving knife (splitter) metal fin behind a circular sawblade to prevent wood catching there

rod a full-sized drawing to lay out dimensions and angles

rowed striped wood with naturally alternating grain direction

sanding block cork or softwood to wrap abrasive paper around for use by hand

sapwood newer growth in outer tree rings, often softer than heartwood

sash cramp (sash clamp) Screwed jaws on long rail for pulling together joints in frames or sash windows

saw bench circular saw with a large metal table

scoring blade small circular sawblade for shallow cut ahead of main blade to prevent splitting

scraper flat steel plate used for fine surface smoothing, especially on difficult grain, sometimes fitted in a plane type-body

scratch stock small scraper for shaping edges or rebating ready to receive inlay

set sideways offset between alternate saw teeth to prevent saw jamming

shaw guard sprung pressure blocks on a machine to hold wood against cutters

site saw lightweight circular saw bench for portable use

skip-tooth bandsaw blade with widely spaced teeth to allow more dust collection in deep cuts

sledge sliding carriage on machine table to carry wood over blades

snatch wood accidentally caught on machine blade and quickly dragged off course

snipe end of board unintentionally reduced in thickness by thicknesser (planer)

spelching (tear-out) wood grain torn from surface or underside

stile vertical rail forming part of a frame

stock wood as a raw material or sliding block on a gauge

substrate groundwork or solid wood beneath veneer

table saw circular saw fitted beneath large flat surface, often cast iron

tail tapered fingers of a dovetail joint

TCT Tungsten Carbide Tipped, hard composite material used for teeth and blade edges

template pattern cut out of board to provide shape for components

tenon peg to be pressed into a mortice to form a joint, usually rectangular

Tersa knife disposable blade for planer (jointer) or thicknesser (planer)

thicknesser (planer) machine for smoothing one side of wood against a reference surface on the other side

through and through sawn (flat-sawn) plain sawn logs converted to boards as a simple series of slices

through dovetail joint where tail fingers are visible on both side and end

through tenon square pegged joint that protrudes right through

timber (lumber) wood as a raw material

timber yard (lumber yard) storage and sales place for converted wood

tpi teeth per inch, a way of expressing the pitch of a saw

tracking adjusting the alignment of bandsaw wheels

try square for checking right angles, thin steel rectangular blade with its end set in a thick rectangular stock

tyre (tire) rubber or similar covering on rim of a bandsaw wheel

vice (vise) screwed jaw fixed to bench for securing wood while working on it

waney natural uneven edge on board formed by outside of the tree left attached

waterstone composite grinding block with hard particulates in a soft base material, to be lubricated with water

wet and dry abrasive paper suitable for lubrication with water, can be used on metals

whetstone grindstone or sharpening stone

Popular woods for furniture-making

Wood	Description and Properties	Sample
Ash	Hardwood. Botanical name: *Fraxinus excelsior* Tough flexible, light in weight, pleasant to work, holds a good finish. White or pale shade of cool pinkish-white. Turns yellow with exposure to light, wax or varnish.	
Ash (Olive)	Same species as normal white ash but some older trees darken in streaks towards the centre. Generally a denser wood but still good to work. Purplish-brown when freshly cut, darkens to brown-black.	
Cedar of Lebanon	Softwood. Botanical name: *Cedrus libani* Light-weight brittle wood with coarse grain. Can be tricky to work especially around knots. Prone to splitting. Strong fresh smell which lasts decades, repellent to most insects.	
Elm	Hardwood. Botanical name: *Ulmus procera* Medium weight, mid-brown rich colour. Quite easy to work but tends to blunt tools. Liable to distorting with moisture. Attractive and varied grain pattern. Prone to woodworm etc.	
Oak (American white)	Hardwood. Botanical name: *Quercus alba* Medium-weight, strong, durable wood. Easy to work. Pale brown, regular mild grain pattern with few knots. Generally good value and dependable but prone to checks (splits) in drying.	
Oak (English or European)	Hardwood. Botanical name: *Quercus robur* Medium to heavy weight, very strong durable wood. Easy to work but prone to large knots and changes in grain direction. Medium brown with strong character.	
Oak (Brown)	Same species as English oak but some trees turn brown when attacked by a bracket fungus. Streaky brown known as tigered oak. Warm attractive colour can add value. Easy to work but base of tree may be softened by fungus.	
Sycamore	Hardwood. Botanical name: *Acer pseudoplatanus* Light to medium weight, pale whitish fine grain. Often rippled pattern is favoured for decorative use. Quite easy to work. Not durable and discolours easily.	
Walnut	Hardwood. Botanical name: *Juglans regia* Medium light-weight, fine-grained wood. Rich varied shades of brown, purple, grey. Excellent to work, cuts crisply and holds fine details and fine finish. Can be prone to checks (splits).	

COMPARISON OF DUST EXTRACTOR FLOW RATES IN DIFFERENT UNITS AND SPEEDS IN DIFFERENT TUBE SIZES

	Cubic metres per hour	Cubic metres per minute	Cubic feet per minute	Litres per second	Litres per minute	Maximum speed down tubes in metres per second		
Common abbreviations	cm/hr $m^3\ hr^{-1}$	cm/m	cfpm cfm	l/s $L\ s^{-1}$	l/m lpm	m/s ms^{-1}		
Tube diameters						100mm	60mm	38mm
	3600	60	2119	1000	60000	127		
	2000	33	1177	556	33333	71		
	1000	17	589	278	16667	35	98	
	600	10	353	167	10000	21	59	
	360	6	212	100	6000	13	35	88
	200	3	118	56	3333	7	20	49
	100	2	59	28	1667	4	10	24
	60	1	35	17	1000	2	6	15
	36	0.6	21	10	600	1.3	4	9
	20	0.3	12	6	333	0.7	2	5

One cubic metre is 1000 litres. One cubic foot is approximately 28 litres

INCHES TO MILLIMETRES

inch		mm	inch		mm	inch		mm
1/64	0.01565	0.3969	11/32	0.34375	8.7312	43/64	0.671875	17.0656
1/32	0.03125	0.7938	23/64	0.359375	9.1281	11/16	0.6875	17.4625
3/64	0.046875	1.1906	3/8	0.375	9.5250	5/64	0.703125	17.8594
1/16	0.0625	1.5875	25/64	0.390625	9.9219	23/32	0.71875	18.2562
5/64	0.078125	1.9844	13/32	0.40625	10.3188	47/64	0.734375	18.6531
3/32	0.09375	2.3812	27/64	0.421875	10.7156	3/4	0.750	19.0500
7/64	0.109375	2.7781	7/16	0.4375	11.1125	49/64	0.765625	19.4469
1/8	0.125	3.1750	29/64	0.453125	11.5094	25/32	0.78125	19.8438
9/64	0.140625	3.5719	15/32	0.46875	11.9062	51/64	0.796875	20.2406
5/32	0.15625	3.9688	31/64	0.484375	12.3031	13/16	0.8125	20.6375
11/64	0.171875	4.3656	1/2	0.500	12.700	53/64	0.828125	21.0344
3/16	0.1875	4.7625	33/64	0.515625	13.0969	27/32	0.84375	21.4312
13/64	0.203125	5.1594	17/32	0.53125	13.4938	55/64	0.858375	21.8281
7/32	0.21875	5.5562	35/64	0.546875	13.8906	7/8	0.875	22.2250
15/64	0.234375	5.9531	9/16	0.5625	14.2875	57/64	0.890625	22.6219
1/4	0.250	6.3500	37/64	0.578125	14.6844	29/32	0.90625	23.0188
17/64	0.265625	6.7469	19/32	0.59375	15.0812	59/64	0.921875	23.4156
9/32	0.28125	7.1438	39/64	0.609375	15.4781	15/16	0.9375	23.8125
19/64	0.296875	7.5406	5/8	0.625	15.8750	61/64	0.953125	24.2094
5/16	0.3125	7.9375	41/64	0.640625	16.2719	31/32	0.96875	24.6062
21/64	0.1328125	8.3344	21/32	0.65625	16.6688	63/64	0.984375	25.0031
						1	1.00	25.4

About the author

John Bullar designs and makes bespoke furniture to commission from his workshop in Cheshire. His style and techniques are contemporary versions of the Arts and Crafts methods his grandfather first used as a cabinetmaker in the 1920s. As a boy, John was taught the skills of furniture-making by his family, although moving to the north coast of Scotland meant the only wood available was from salvage and recycling. After graduating in Engineering at Leeds University he took a career in design and then industrial safety.

With their own children grown up, John and his wife Chris decided to get back into the furniture-making business, first gaining commissions through local word of mouth then, with the help of the internet, growing a wide base of clients.

John regularly writes project and technical articles, published by UK and US magazines as well as translated into other languages. Belonging to a group of designer-makers, he visits workshops across the country, comparing techniques with some of the finest makers. Listening and talking to clients about new ideas, working with fine native hardwoods and using good tools continue to give John much pleasure and satisfaction with his craft.

For more information, visit John's website at:
www.bullar.co.uk

Index